KAREN WAS STARING INTENTLY AT HILDEGARD.
HER EYES WERE WIDE, AS IF STARING INTO THE
POOR GIRL'S SOUL AND SEARCHING FOR SECRETS.
AFTER A LITTLE WHILE, KAREN ABRUPTLY SPOKE UP.

"YOU'RE IN LOVE, AREN'T YOU?"

"WH-HUHWHAT?!"

HILDEGARD SHRIEKED, SHRINKING BACK AS CRIMSON
SHOT ACROSS HER CHEEKS.
HER COMPOSED EXPRESSION WAS COMPLETELY OBLITERATED,
REPLACED BY A PROFUSELY SWEATING BROW AND PANICKED EYES.

In Another World With My Smartphone 7

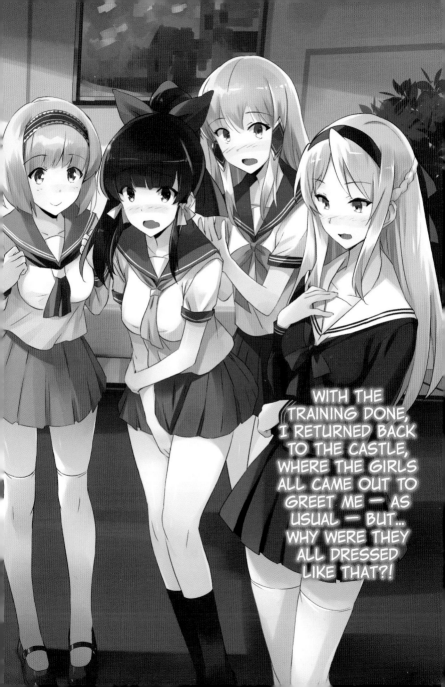

WITH THE TRAINING DONE, I RETURNED BACK TO THE CASTLE, WHERE THE GIRLS ALL CAME OUT TO GREET ME — AS USUAL — BUT... WHY WERE THEY ALL DRESSED LIKE THAT?!

"HERE, IT'S A FRAME GEAR WITH A FOCUS ON MOBILITY. I CALL IT THE DRAGOON."

"WOAH! IT'S RED, THAT'S COOL."

ENDE LAZILY TOSSED THE SLIDE OVER TO ME AND CLIMBED UP ONTO THE DRAGON KNIGHT. THE HATCH OPENED UP AND HE CLAMBERED ON IN.

In Another World With My Smartphone

Patora Fuyuhara
illustration·Eiji Usatsuka

IN ANOTHER WORLD WITH MY SMARTPHONE: VOLUME 7
by Patora Fuyuhara

Translated by Andrew Hodgson
Edited by DxS

Original Japanese edition published in 2016 by Hobby Japan
This English edition is published by arrangement with Hobby Japan, Tokyo

English translation © 2018 J-Novel Club LLC

Find more books like this one at www.j-novel.club!

President and Publisher: Samuel Pinansky
Managing Editor: Aimee Zink

ISBN: 978-1-7183-5006-9
Printed in Korea
First Printing: December 2019
10 9 8 7 6 5 4 3 2 1

Contents

Chapter I	Calamity	9
Chapter II	The Knight Princess' First Love	105
Chapter III	The Pruning	142
Interlude	A Myriad of Love	234

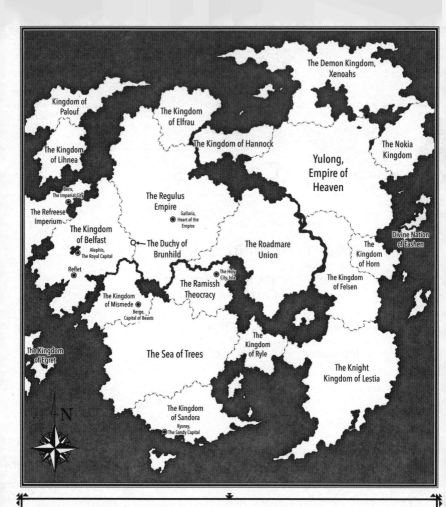

The Story So Far!

Touya received territory from the Kingdom of Belfast and the Regulus Empire, and he christened the new land the Duchy of Brunhild! With the aid of his vassals, and the legacy of an ancient era, he's slowly cultivating a force that can repel the Phrase, otherworldly invaders sent to wreak havoc upon the world! Along with his newfound allies and his trusty divine Smartphone, his unorthodox adventures as a Grand Duke continue! But, lurking in the shadows, there are those that covet his power... Those that would do anything to seize what he has.

In total, I'd gathered together six Babylons. They were the garden, the workshop, the alchemy lab, the hangar, the rampart, and the tower.

Initially there were fifteen mini-robots working in the rampart, but I diverted ten of them to the hangar in order to give Monica and Rosetta some much-needed aid. They were thankful for the reduced workload.

I brought Liora and Noel to Zanac's dressing room, and told them they could choose anything they liked. Liora picked a blazer, while Noel chose a jersey. *Why'd you choose that of all things? Ah, whatever… I guess if they like it, then that's fine.*

The day had finally come for Brunhild's guild hall to finish construction, so I wandered over to give it an inspection.

For the most part, the place was ready for a grand opening. It just needed furniture and decorations on the inside. I was especially impressed with the craftsmanship. Apparently people were quite eager and passionate about the guild hall being opened, because it was one in a territory belonging to a grand duke who had his roots in guild adventuring.

I thought that was fine, but I didn't really expect too many adventurers to show up. Brigands and monsters weren't common in Brunhild, so I figured most of the quests wouldn't be anything adventurous.

Hell, the place was smack-bang in the middle of Regulus and Belfast, so it wouldn't have surprised me much if we didn't get any monster-killing quests at all.

Samsa the ogre was still hard at work, this time helping to build the nearby bar. Only the bar's framework was built, so there was still a fair bit for him to do. He was much too big to help out with any of the guild hall's indoor furnishing, after all.

"Hm…" I suddenly looked over to see Sakura gazing at the construction works. Sango and Kokuyou were by her side, swimming through the air.

"Heyyy! Nice to ssseee you, darling."

"…Lord." Sakura still hadn't recovered her memories, but I could hardly just kick her out. I decided it'd be best to let her stay in the castle as my guest.

Despite her quiet nature, she was actually quite active and outgoing. I asked Sango and Kokuyou to accompany her just in case she found herself in trouble or wandered off too far.

"What brings you guys here?"

"We were at Moon Reader until jussst a while ago. We were walking home, but when we got here, the girl sssimply ssstopped moving and began ssstaring." Kokuyou answered my question, rather than Sakura.

"You guys were at Moon Reader? Who paid for the food?"

"The manager just said it'd be fine putting it on your tab." *Tsk… That's annoying, even by her standards. Then again, the Moon Reader branch over here is pretty much a store operated by the government, so it's fine…*

"So what's Sakura doing now, exactly?"

"Watching…" Sakura suddenly murmured something, and pointed over at Samsa the ogre. He was hauling timber with a big smile on his face. *What, something on his face?*

"He's demonkin… but nobody minds… It's strange."

Ah, I see… so that's what's got her curious. I'll admit, it's definitely weird for demonkin to work together peacefully with humans. In most cases, humans are scared of demonkin and their ilk, which makes both species avoid the other.

Outside of Brunhild, I hadn't witnessed another place where man and demonkin laughed together, or shared drinks together. Whenever I saw demonkin in other countries, they were mostly on their own, in the corners of bars and such.

"Demonkin or not, my country doesn't tolerate discrimination. It's true that travelers from other countries might steer clear of them, but there are even five demonkin members of my knight order. We're quite diverse."

"This country is strange… It shifts to the whims of its leader… Still, it's nice here… Everyone here wishes to work in harmony, together." I got the feeling she wasn't really praising me, but I was happy nonetheless.

Well, Brunhild was a rather small country, so it was only natural that everyone worked hard together to make a future.

I decided to take Sakura over to look at the agricultural project in the east of Brunhild. Lakshy the alraune was hard at work in the fields as usual. She was demonkin, too.

"What're you raising here, then?"

"Radishes and turnips! They'll be ready for harvest soon, I'm sure. We should pickle 'em. They're super yummy when you do that." Lakshy smiled as she spoke. Apparently the pickling method was

11

something unique to Eashen, but it was spreading across Brunhild quickly due to most of our citizens being Eashenese.

The rice paddies were coming along well too. I wanted to expand the project until spring. I was looking forward to chowing down on some rice.

After that we should grow miso and soybeans, all the good stuff for natto. Tofu and green beans sound good too. I was getting a bit excited, so I hoped for spring to come a bit sooner.

We said our goodbyes to Lakshy and started back down the road to the castle.

After a while of walking, something felt strange. There was nobody around, nobody in the area but us.

"Massster…"

"I know." Sango spoke up to warn me, but I was already deploying a **[Shield]**. It was just in time for an arrow to come flying at us from a nearby tree.

"Ah…?!" Sakura took a sharp, surprised breath, but the spell successfully deflected the attack. I looked up to the place the arrow came from, and saw someone clad in a black mask, kind of like the type used in traditional Chinese theater.

That's a weird-looking mask… It's definitely suspicious. I walked toward the tree, only to be ambushed where I stood by three similar, black-clad men from the ground. I'd sensed several presences in the area, but I was surprised they'd been buried in the soil. They carried curved shortswords. I narrowed my eyes and took a closer look at the unusual blades. They were slicked with a liquid, likely poison.

There was no mistaking it. I was face-to-face with a group of assassins.

"Tell us the whereabouts of the Giant Warrior."

"…The Giant Warrior? You mean my Frame Gear?"

"Silence. Answer."

"No. I don't answer to you. What country are you from?" I spoke clearly to the three in front of me, but they didn't respond. It would've been fine if they'd just been obedient and answered me, but they had to make it hard. I walked over and quickly tapped all three of them on the shoulder.

"[Gravity]."

"Guwagh?!" I made them bow at my feet using my weight-altering magic. Horrified by the display, the fourth assassin leaped out of the tree and started running away.

"[Slip]."

"Guwah?!" The fourth assassin fell to the ground immediately. He smacked the back of his head pretty hard. *Ouch, poor timing…*

I decided to leave that guy for now, and focused my attention on the three men in front of me. I reached down to pull their masks off. *Let's see what you look like…*

"Don't!" Sakura suddenly charged toward me and yanked my arm away. I fell flat on my back… just as the three men burst into flames. Their masks detonated.

"A-Ah…" The three men slumped to the ground, motionless. Chunks of flesh danced through the air alongside smoke. Their heads had been blown off completely.

What the hell was that? A suicide bomb tactic in case they got caught? I'd seen some historical plays where ninja would bite their tongues out if they got caught, but this was a little much…

Then again, suicide bombing pretty much guaranteed death. If their tongues came off, they could still be kept alive and tortured.

I looked over at the guy I'd tripped over, but he wasn't there anymore. A weapon similar to a kunai dagger attached to rope was lodged into a nearby tree. [Slip] affected an area on the ground, so he must've pulled himself out of the operational area.

I looked around for his mask, but I didn't find it. He'd likely disposed of it and made his getaway. I didn't understand what had just happened, but I knew I needed to take countermeasures before they came back for a second go. I decided to meet this mysterious challenge head-on.

"I didn't find any identifying documents or features on the three corpses, and one of the men got away. Thus, he is unaccounted for." Vice-Commander Nikola read his report out to me. I didn't want it to become an especially major matter, but it was true that the monarch of a nation had come under direct attack, so I couldn't keep quiet about it.

The people joining me in the conference room were the top three members of the knight order, Prime Minister Kousaka, the old men from Takeda, and Tsubaki of the intel corps.

"So then… were they after somethin' of yours, squirt?"

"I'm pretty sure, yeah… I have no doubts they were after the Frame Gear."

"Guess that means we gotta suspect every other country, then." Old man Baba sighed and folded his arms as he leaned back into chair.

I could understand where he was coming from. The Frame Gear was something seen as a potent weapon by other countries, so I wasn't surprised another group finally made a move to try and gain it. They were likely aiming to kidnap and torture me until I told them where it was.

The arrow the fourth guy fired was probably coated in poison, too. It was probably paralysis-inducing, and they'd smeared it on their swords to make sure they could cart me off easily.

"It's unlikely that a nation affiliated with our western alliance would've done such a thing. And even if it was, it's entirely possible that it was the careless action of an influential noble, rather than the government of the country itself. We must not take brash action without understanding full well who the culprit is." I agreed with Kousaka's assessment. If a country from the western alliance tried to steal from me, the other nations would vilify them. It would've been suicide to make a move like that.

Plus, they'd called it the Giant Warrior. That meant they didn't know it was called a Frame Gear. It was far more likely that the assassination attempt was performed by a country I hadn't involved myself with yet.

As I pondered, Tsubaki raised her hand.

"Excuse me, there's a matter I was concerned with. You said they were wearing masks, which stood out to me a tad."

"Why's that strange? No matter the era, spy groups and assassination teams always wear masks. Is there something odd about it?"

"No, I was just thinking… If we knew a bit more about the mask, it might help us identify them…"

Well, that's a fair point… But those masks have all been blown to smithereens. Lapis and Cecile used masks when they worked for Belfast's Intelligence Task Force, Espion… If what Yamagata had said was true, and every organization used a mask… then it may have been possible to identify them from the mask.

"What did the masks look like?"

"Uh… kinda similar in style to those used in traditional Chinese theater."

"Chinese?" Commander Lain tilted her head in confusion. Her rabbit ears twitched just as curiously. *Oh, right... other world. Oh, I know.*

I took out a piece of paper from a desk and used **[Drawing]**. I depicted a perfectly accurate replica of what the masks on my assailants looked like.

"...Feels a tad late for me to say it, but you sure have a lot of convenient stuff at your disposal, Milord." Vice-Commander Norn muttered quietly. *Well, just call it Your Majesty's magic... heh.*

"That's the mask, anyway. Recognize it?" Everyone stared down at the image, until eventually Tsubaki spoke up.

"I've no proof, but the coloring and markings here are... reminiscent of Yulong's national symbols. I'd heard rumors that there's a spy organization named "Qulau" operating out of that nation."

"Yulong?"

"Yulong, Empire of Heaven. It's a country west of Eashen, over the sea. They've warred against Eashen many a time, and are governed by the heavenly emperor." *Huh... Yulong, Empire of Heaven? They're Eashen's neighbors from across the sea, eh? It's quite a way away... If the assailants did come from there, they traveled far.*

Well, not like I have any proof it's them. It's probably better to act cautiously though... I doubt they'll give up after one attempt.

For the time being I decided to bolster defenses and make sure people paid attention to suspicious things. I assumed their plan was to steal the Frame Gear, and there was no way in hell I planned on letting them have it.

The only way to Babylon was either through one of my portals, or the short-range recall teleport that Cesca and the other Gynoids had.

There was always the chance they could get there by launching into the sky and hoping for the best, but that wouldn't be an issue. Ever since I obtained the rampart, directly invading from the outside had become an impossibility.

I didn't much care if they sent people after me, but I couldn't avoid the possibility of them targeting my loved ones. To that end, I decided it'd be better to send them a message suggesting I wasn't to be messed with.

If they *did* end up going after the people I cared about, then I wouldn't forgive them. I'd mercilessly hunt down the ringleader and make him wish he was dead.

Still, the people who came after me blew themselves up to conceal their identities. The guy in charge was probably a real monster.

Come to think of it... How come Sakura knew they were gonna blow up? She isn't from that spy agency or something, is she...? Nah, that can't be. I found her in Eashen, not Yulong, and Yumina's Mystic Eyes have confirmed her status as non-malicious.

Though that begged the question, the Mystic Eyes might not be able to account for bad people who had lost their memories.

It was hard to know if a bad person who, upon losing their memories and becoming like a whole other person, would still be judged as evil. I had no idea about the mechanics of it, exactly, and it was a little too philosophical for my tastes, so I left it there.

I felt a little anxious about the day Sakura's memories would return.

Still, I decided to push those anxieties aside. Sakura wasn't a bad girl, surely.

"Alright, here I go…"

"Sure thing." I was at the training grounds with Linze, who pointed a mithril rod at me. It had various spellstones fit on the tip. Of the three stones, red, blue, and yellow, the red one shone brightly.

"Come forth, Fire! Hail of Red Stones: [Ignis Fire]!" A flaming orb about the size of a baseball flew out of the rod. She'd cast a basic fire spell.

I watched it approaching, focused my magic, and cast my new Null spell.

"[Absorb]." The fireball dispersed like a fine mist. It didn't hit me, so I was completely unharmed.

Another shot came flying at me. However, just like the one before it, it dispersed into nothingness. *Hm… guess it's on a timer, then… This spell eats up a lot of magic, but it makes up for that by absorbing any offensive magic around me.*

"Linze, step it up a notch."

"Very well." Linze readied her rod once more.

"Come forth, Fire! Purgatorial Pillar: [Inferno Fire]!"

"[Absorb]." Three billowing torrents of flame came at me from multiple angles. But, once they got about two meters away from me, they vanished as well.

Hm…? Well, my magic got restored, but… it's only about the same amount as the fireball gave me. Guess it must return a fixed amount, which means the spell I drain is irrelevant… The spell gets canceled out, turned back into raw magic, then part of that is absorbed. Pretty neat.

The effect was similar to the Drainbracer used during the coup, so I was certain I could enchant items with it as well.

I asked Linze if I could see about making magic absorbing armor, but Linze said it'd be pointless. Apparently if someone absorbed spells from schools other than the ones they had the attributes for, then they could get something called spellsickness.

So if a person had no aptitude for fire magic and absorbed a fire spell, they'd be negatively affected. It wouldn't be an issue for someone like me, but the average person wasn't so well-attuned. Apparently the Drainbracer didn't seem to have that problem, though.

Linze and Yumina were both only attuned to three magic schools, but Leen would probably be able to absorb all magic except Darkness. She was attuned to all other schools, after all.

She could also use **[Transfer]** to give magic to others.

"Guess it won't help much for being caught off-guard, though, since you've gotta manually invoke it."

"What's the range on it?"

"Uh, it's around two to ten meters, I think. Oh, that brings up an interesting question... Would an enemy within that range even be able to cast a spell to begin with?" I kept Linze standing next to me and triggered **[Absorb]**. She cast her spell and it activated for about half a second before being nullified.

Huh, so I guess I could preemptively keep it cast on me. When Linze left the effective range, she could cast normally once more.

The spell was one that completely nullified magic entirely. **[Silence]** only stopped spells from being chanted because it stopped the sound itself, and I could use **[Taboo]** to seal certain words in advance if I knew what spells my enemy was using. It was useful if I knew my enemy, but wouldn't be much use in a real fight.

Then again, knowing my enemy would certainly help in some cases. For example, if I made **[Boost]** a taboo word and I had to fight Elze, it'd certainly be to my advantage.

Regardless, none of these spells would do me any good against a Phrase.

The experiment was complete. I thanked Linze for her help and set off toward home when suddenly I received a telepathic message from Kohaku.

《My lord, we've a visitor at the castle...》

《A visitor?》

《Er, yes... She's calling herself your older sister...》

《Excuse me?!》

What older sister? I don't have any sisters... I don't even have any brothers! I've got cousins from my mother's sister, and my dad's older brother went through that wedding and divorce, but none of those people would be in this world, either.

《What does the person look like?》

《Ah, well... She's pink-haired and looks to be around half a decade older than you, and she— Wh-Wh-What is she doing?! Agh! 》

《Hmhm? What's this, Kohaku? Ehehe, it's a telepathic connection, is it? Then I'll talk with Touya too, get it? Heeey, can you hear me, dear?》 The amused voice of a young woman came mixed in on Kohaku's wavelength. The voice was strangely familiar.

Wait... no. Oh no... What the hell are you doing here?! I opened up a **[Gate]** and rushed to the castle immediately, dragging Linze off with me.

"I'm Touya's biiig sister! You can call me Karen, get it?"

"Karen, was it?" She spoke up, greeting everyone like it was no big deal. *What the hell are you saying? You're not even a human!*

I approached her and let out a quiet whisper.

"...God of love, what exactly are you doing in my castle?"

"I'm not the god of love, get it? I'm Karen! It'll be fine if you call me big sis... Actually, make sure to call me that, get it?!"

That's not an answer to my question at all!

"I'm so happy to see you after so long! Hehehe, hurray!"

"Gaugh!" She suddenly pulled me into a tight embrace. *Hey now, everyone's watching!* I glanced over at Yumina and the others, but they seemed to be touched. From their perspective, it was the long-awaited reunion of a brother and his beloved sister, after all. Yae was even shedding a few tears. This was bad...

"Well then... venerable sister-in-law, allow us to take our leave. We'll ensure you're fed well tonight, so please look forward to it."

"Oh my! I am looking forward to it, get it?" I guess they wanted to give the 'two siblings' time to reconcile. Eventually it was only the god of love and myself.

"So, what's going on? Why'd you come down to the mortal realm?"

"Huh... Shouldn't I have come?"

"No! I don't mean like that, I just wonder why you're posing as my sister!"

"Oh, it was just an idea of mine, get it…?" The god of love reclined on the couch with a little chuckle. I was mentally exhausted at this point, so I sat down too. *This is bad… This girl isn't the kind of person I handle very well…*

"So, what's the deal? Why're you here?"

"Hoho… I came to catch someone, get it?"

"Huh? You mean like capturing someone?"

"That's right! We're lesser gods, but I'm here to capture a god even lower down the ladder! A servile god, to be precise! The naughty little fellow escaped and came down here, get it? So I came down to get them back, get it?" *A servile god? Didn't know you could get lesser than lesser.*

From what I understood the gods had a strict hierarchy, so servile gods must have been placed under gods of specific concepts. This one must've ran away and come to this world for whatever reason.

"You said he escaped? Did he commit a crime up there or something?"

"Nope! There wasn't anything like a crime, get it? I've no idea why the little dear came down here. That being said, coming to a lower world without the World God's permission is actually a crime in and of itself, but it should be fine so long as the god in question doesn't influence the world with their divine powers. That's why I'm worried, get it?"

…I think you're interfering plenty already in a broader sense… You're the one who made me peek on Yumina and the others when they were changing!

"Gods like me can come and go without an issue. If you want me to put it in easy terms, I'm a driver with a perfectly valid license, get it? But a servile god isn't licensed, nor do they have a temporary license, so they're like a child in the driver's seat! It's quite a dangerous situation, get it?"

I guess I get it, but at the same time I don't fully understand. In the end, it's bad not to be licensed, I guess.

"Then go out and catch the guy already. I don't want any trouble."

"That's the plan, geez! But I haven't been able to feel any of their Divine Essence since I got here… They probably transformed into something that exists here already."

"Eh? Transformed?"

"Yep! Could be a person, an animal, or maybe even something like an object or plant! It's a technique to blend in. So long as it's active, the natural divinity they emanate is inert, get it?"

Huh, weird. That's definitely troubling, though…

It would be bad news for everyone if the god started using his powers. A god was still a god, no matter the tier. I hoped he'd be caught and brought to justice swiftly. Still, the fact that we didn't know why he'd come down to this world, coupled with the fact that he was concealing himself was definitely troubling.

"So what're you gonna do to find him?"

"The moment that servile god uses a single bit of divine power, I'll know where they are! Then, we can undo the transformation with our own divine power after finding out where they are, get it?"

"Uh, our?"

Hey hey, you didn't bring ANOTHER god down here, did you? I remember the god of swords, the god of agriculture, and the god of music being mentioned… Curse that careless old man!

"What do you mean? I'm talking about you, get it? You have magical power and divine power, silly. How do you think I even found you in the first place? I can smell the godliness on you as well as I can see the cleanliness!"

"Seriously?!" *Wait a sec… Is this one of the bodily changes I'll be undergoing? I didn't even know about it!*

"Well, I won't be able to do anything until they make a move, get it? So… with that saiiid… thanks for having me here, little bro."

"Wait, you're gonna stay here?!" *Seriously? Well, I mean… I'll be worrying about that god until he reveals himself, so having her here might not be the worst thing… But I don't really trust having this girl of all people hanging around!*

"There's no problems with an older sister coming to stay with her younger brother, get it?"

"Hm, older sister, eh? Makes me wonder just how old you are…" I tried to tease her, but she just puffed her cheeks out and glared daggers at me. Asking her age seemed an unwise idea, so I decided not to push it, lest she cast me into a living hell.

"Anyhow, just call me Sissy-wissy. That's the best way, get it?"

"…No way am I calling you that."

"If you don't, I might accidentally tell Yumina and the others all about that time you came to ask me for help with your love troubles… get it?"

"Ah, please accept my apologies, S-Sissy-wissy…" *Curse it all… Is this the legendary power of a god at play?* Calling her… that, was far too embarrassing, so I got her to compromise on calling her Sis instead. The god of love… or well, Karen, seemed a little disappointed, but she accepted my terms.

I kinda wondered what was going through the old man's head when he assigned her to this job, though. I had no idea if she was the right kind of person for it.

The meal that evening was nothing short of extravagant. Crea had clearly put her all into making it a grand feast.

But then… during dinner, something bad and uncomfortable happened. They started asking her for love advice. She was a pro, after all… No, beyond that, really… but it didn't make it any less unpleasant to endure during my meal. Yumina and the others began to ask her things, one by one.

"Touya's the kind of person who's inherently kind, get it? From a woman's perspective, that can be kind of cruel, though… They might see it as him hitting on them, or displaying interest when really he's just a gentle soul… It'd be bad if they misunderstood his intentions, get it?"

"B-But doesn't that mean he's not especially fond of us either? He treats us all so kindly, but it's all the same…" Linze muttered.

"No no, that's not the case… He considers all of you to be precious, get it? But it's up to you girls to decide how that progresses. He's not the kind to make a move on his own, so you're the ones who have to gently push."

"So we just need to be more aggressive?" Elze asked.

"In moderation… He'll only become more flustered if you attack too strongly, get it? Touya's the kind of boy who gets very shy very easily."

"Th-Then just how far is far enough…?"

"First thing's physical contact… Hugging, kissing, and holding hands is good, get it? Slowly whittling away at his shyness by doing stuff like this often is key. It'll eventually become second nature, get it? My my, you must all be having a tough time, eh? What inexperienced girls you are… It's so cute."

"Wh-What about, erm… seduction…?" Yumina inquired.

"Be careful about how far you go, there… Too many naughty things might end up giving him mental fatigue… Start up by wearing shorter skirts to tease him… But only do that in front of

Touya! If another person gets a peek of your panties, he'll hate it for sure!"

"I see... This is most intriguing..." Yae mumbled. *Please put an end to this, I'm begging you! What the hell kind of shameless conversation is this?! This isn't romantic advice anymore!* I looked around the table and noticed Renne was also listening attentively. Meanwhile, the men at the table just looked at me with solemn eyes. They seemed to understand how tough I had it.

I'm getting embarrassed here, come on! Get me outta here! And that's how one of the very worst people possible became my older sister.

"Wait, Yulong declared war?"

"That's correct, yes. They declared war on their neighboring nation, the Hannock Kingdom, and are currently planning to mount an offensive." As Tsubaki gave me her report, I took my smartphone out and got a good look at the area around Yulong.

The Kingdom of Hannock was west of Yulong, and bordered Regulus along a large river. On the map, I could see that the territory they controlled was more horizontal than vertical.

"Run search. Display Yulong's forces in red, and Hannock's in blue."

"Understood. Displaying." Just like that, it showed the lot. They were split up into a neat color code.

My search magic was definitely a handy information gathering application. It couldn't be used on people who disguised their features or changed clothes, like the masked assailants from the other day, but it was pretty easy to look for general concepts and locations.

We didn't find a single trace of those black masks, either. I figured they'd blown up to the last trace in order to prevent any possibility of being identified.

According to the map, there were two Yulong war camps within Hannock's territory. There was another large group of Yulong forces headed toward both camps, which I figured was probably a resupply unit. Either way, the situation seemed to be in Yulong's favor. They were advancing forward with overwhelming numbers.

"Why did war even break out?"

"Yulong's official stance is that Hannock was originally Yulong's territory, and that refugees had settled there and made their own kingdom many years ago without proper permission. They're stating it's not war, just a reclamation of rightful soil."

"...Is that how it works?"

"That's how they're saying it works. They say that Yulong has prospered since before recorded time. They claim that Yulong has an empire spanning 7000 years. It's handed down as an oral tradition over there." *7000 years? That's crazy. Even Egypt only has a history spanning 5000 years, right...?* I could understand that they were trying to take back their ancestral territory, but there was already another country there now with people living peacefully in it. I couldn't help but wonder why they chose now of all times to reclaim it. And I didn't quite understand the whole oral tradition thing, either. I turned to Cesca, who was standing by my side, and spoke to her in a quiet voice.

"...Hey uh, during the ancient era 5000 years ago... was there a country called Yulong?"

"Nope. I haven't heard of anything like that. All human nations were ravaged by the Phrase and rendered uninhabitable during their final push."

Hmhmhm... So Yulong's proud 7000 years of tradition doesn't sound so legit after all. If I have to hazard a guess, I'd say some influential people started a cool story about their history and spread it to future generations as the truth. But if that's the case, then it casts the entire Hannock situation into doubt, too... Well, I can't discredit everything Yulong says based on this. They probably actually believe this stuff because they were taught it for so many generations.

"If you'd like my opinion, the war was begun under false pretenses. Over the last few years, Hannock has discovered a wealth of ore. They've become much more economically powerful due to their mithril and orichalcum reserves. In my humble opinion, it is this wealth that is driving Yulong's bloodlust."

Wait, they're being aggressive for resources? Surely Yulong isn't seeing it as some bounty to be claimed, right...? Though it does add up... They allegedly attacked me looking for the Frame Gear the other day. Are they the kind of people that pump money into their military, trample the enemy, and then use their resources and technology to bolster their own might?

"Guh... A war is kind of a first for me... How does the situation look?"

"Yulong has the advantage when it comes to raw military might. If it continues as it is, Hannock will likely be destroyed. It might be possible for them to bolster their troops using the funds from their ore mines, but the difference in strength between Hannock and Yulong is just too big for it to even be a fair contest."

If they destroy Hannock, would Yulong go after Regulus too? That definitely wouldn't be good news...

This coupled with the attack on Brunhild the other day wasn't painting me the brightest picture of Yulong. Though it wasn't confirmed that they were the attackers, so I reserved judgment.

"Does the Kingdom of Hannock have much in the way of relations with Regulus?"

"They're associated, but not allied. They definitely maintain a friendly relationship. In regards to the current war, however, Regulus will not intervene. They may provide aid in the form of food or arms, but not much else."

Hmph... If it goes on like that, the war will just be prolonged. Even then, it's not like it'd be hard for Yulong to win if Hannock had more support.

It's a foreign, unrelated war... It has nothing to do with me... If I could think with that mindset, it'd be easier.

A lot of people are gonna die... I'm hardly a humanitarian, I have my own things to take care of... But I can't help but feel rotten when I imagine the deaths of those people, regardless of whether or not they know me.

I couldn't decide if that was hypocritical or heroic.

My late grandfather once told me "Better a hypocrite than a bystander!" and that "If you stand and stare like a monkey, you might as well be one!"

...And honestly? I don't want to be a monkey.

"Oh, that reminds me. Weren't there members of our knight order from Yulong or Hannock?"

"We have nobody from Yulong amongst our ranks. However, there is one soldier who was born in Hannock."

"Call him here, then. I wish to speak with him."

"As you wish." Tsubaki swiftly left the room.

*If he's from Hannock, then he might have family still living there...
It'd be better to bring them here to Brunhild if that place is gonna get
wrecked soon.*

"Knight Paolo reporting for duty, sir!" The knight I had called
over bowed his head to me and stood on one knee. He was a young
man with short, auburn hair. I'd seen him a few times here and there.
If I recalled correctly, he was fast on his feet, but not especially skilled
at swordplay. Either way, he was diligent, so Nikola had remarked on
his abilities every now and then.

Apparently he was originally a regular adventurer, and came
here to sign up after seeing a recruitment flyer.

"Paolo, you hail from Hannock, yes? Where is your hometown,
exactly?"

"Er... Ah, well. My hometown is a small village named Quint,
which is on the eastern side of Hannock. Why do you..." *Quint
Village...* I called up my map and displayed the location.

*Oh, that's not good. Yulong's army is a little close for comfort...
Are they gonna conquer this village and use it as their base of
operations or something? They're aiming for Hannock's capital for
the most part, but there's a smaller group heading for Quint... Are
they trying to make a pincer attack or something? Invading army or
not, surely they won't kill villagers. But that doesn't mean they won't
take provisions and general supplies... It's just a matter of whether the
villagers give them over peacefully or not.*

"Er, sorry... What is this?" Paolo stared at me with a look of
anxiety on his face. He looked between me and the map, then
pointed at the location of his town on the projection.

"The news isn't formally out yet, but... Yulong has declared war
on Hannock."

"What are you saying?!" Paolo stood up straight, clearly shocked. He had anxiety, surprise, and a twinge of horror painted on his face.

"This here is Quint Village... And the red marks here are Yulong's forces. It's looking like they'll reach Quint by morning."

"B-But..." Paolo stared at my map, equal parts horrified and amazed.

"So long as the villagers don't act rashly, I'm sure things will be okay, but—"

"...No, you don't understand. E-Everyone in Quint, my family... and friends... They're all going to die, or worse. The men will be slaughtered, and the women and children will definitely be taken to be slaves and playthings...!"

"What?!"

Hold on a sec... is he kidding? They're formal soldiers, right? If they acted like raiders, they'd just be common criminals. They can't seriously get away with that, right?

"Yulong's army is infamous for their heinous behavior, Milord... When they invade another country, they're permitted to pillage at their own discretion. They can take weapons and armor from fallen foes, they can take money and jewels that they find in people's houses... They can even take women to claim as property... It's because of this reason that Yulong's army has some of the highest morale in the world."

He can't be serious... If they act like that, they'll just make the locals hate them! If they're invading to make the land theirs, then what are they planning?

"Twenty or so years ago, there was a country called Zaram between Hannock and Yulong... It was savagely destroyed by Yulong's forces. There were widespread reports of pillaging and rape during that time."

...No matter the circumstances of war, there's no need for soldiers to go that far!

According to Tsubaki, Yulong held a strong caste system, and your social status was determined by one simple detail, whether or not you're a native Yulongese person. Their xenophobia was extremely strong, and they viewed outsiders as lesser beings.

Slavery was apparently common in Yulong as well, much like Sandora. But they didn't use collars. Instead, they denoted slaves with special tattoos.

"It's likely that Quint village will be completely ravaged, just as Zaram was before... Gh... Milord, I-I'm so sorry to speak out of line like this, but... I beg of you! Please, use your power to save my home!" Paolo knelt down again, bowing and crying out to me.

"Sure."

"Milord, I know... I know how rude this is, but I beseech you, please! Give your most honorable of considerations to saving m— Wait..." Paolo raised his head, dumbfounded.

"What's wrong? I said I'd do it, didn't I? The only reason I called you here was to help anyway."

Well, the original plan was just to evacuate Paolo's family. I figured that would be an easy enough job, and I didn't really expect the village to be in any real danger...

"I don't know if they'll believe me even if I explain it outright, so could you come along to the village with me?"

"Y-Yes sir, of course!" I used [**Recall**] to receive Paolo's memories of Quint, and we went there immediately through a [**Gate**].

It was just the three of us. Myself, Tsubaki, and Paolo.

I opened my eyes to see a peaceful and beautiful little village.

"This is Quint, then?"

"Y-Yes, it is… This is definitely where I was born. Your magic is incredible… To move so far, so quickly…" Paolo made a dumbfounded face at his surroundings, but he seemed relieved.

A young man, who looked like a farmer, called out to us.

"Paolo? Huh, that you, Paolo?"

"Holy cow! Lent? It's been forever, man!" Paolo ran over to the young farmer. They seemed to be friends, or at least acquaintances.

"What's with that getup? Did you loot it off a dead guy or something?"

"You dumbass! I'm totally a knight of Brunhild, bro. I didn't steal a thing. I'm a certified soldier under a grand duke!"

"Whoa, for reals?" Paolo proudly jerked a thumb toward his mithril armor. I noticed that his way of speaking had switched pretty quickly. He sounded a lot more casual and confident in himself.

"Pfft. You used to be famous for your getaway speed. You doing well in your new job with those skills, wahaha…"

"Heh, maybe, maybe… Wait, there's no time for idle banter! Yulong and Hannock are at war with each other now!" Lent's face suddenly grew sullen at Paolo's proclamation.

"Yeah, we know… Everyone's worried. We should be alright since we're quite a way off the main highway, but if the capital falls and Yulong takes over, life'll change a lot…"

"No, that's not it! Yulong's army is coming here right now! They'll be here before the morning!"

"What the hell are you even saying?! That's impossible! There's no reason for them to attack a little village like this… We have barely any food or goods as it is." It was as I'd expected. The army en route to the village was a detached force, likely part of some grander strategy. While the two main forces stared each other down on the highway, Yulong had support armies going the long way around... probably.

"Bring us to the village chief. His Highness here'll help us!"

"Er, His Highness?"

"I told you, I work for a country now, the Duchy of Brunhild. This man here is the grand duke himself!"

"Uh, hi..." Paolo made several exaggerated hand motions as he introduced me. However, his actions were too sudden, so I just gave a small nod.

Lent blinked slowly, and then turned to face Paolo with concern.

"Paolo... Are you okay?" Just as I'd expected, he didn't believe me. I began seriously considering constructing a crown just to wear for such occasions.

Either way, eventually we got Lent to take us to the village chief. I wasn't too surprised he doubted us. It was a lot to stomach after all.

When I went out, I typically dressed in adventurer clothing since it was easy to move in. Plus, wearing gaudy royal clothing wasn't really my scene. Frankly, that stuff made me embarrassed.

We met with the village chief, but he didn't believe us either. He accepted that I was Brunhild's leader, but he just couldn't believe that Yulong's army was headed this way.

I used [**Levitate**] alongside [**Fly**] to bring the chief up in the air with me. Then, I flew toward the approaching forces.

We looked down from the sky, giving him a clear view of the incoming Yulong army. There were a lot of them. I'd have wagered around 5000 or so. At the sight, the village chief shivered and groaned. I couldn't tell whether it was out of shock or fear of heights, though.

We landed, and I used **[Gate]** to send him back to the village. I asked him to talk to the other villagers while I flew around the surrounding area.

I pulled out my map and noted my observations. There was the main force on the highway, and the detached unit headed for the village, but there was also another separate unit trailing behind the main one. I assumed them to be the resupply unit, but there were a lot of them too.

I looked over at Hannock's forces, and they simply paled in comparison. There weren't many troops that weren't already part of the main group. I zoomed the map out and saw another force coming from behind Hannock's main army. They looked like reinforcements coming from Hannock's capital. By my estimations, it'd take about two days for them to reach the main forces. They seemed to be wanting to hold the front line...

What should I do about that... I kind of need a just cause if I want to interfere with a foreign war. I'd prefer to make the Yulong army retreat, but that won't end the war. They'll just come back. It'd be easier if they were attacking Brunhild... Then I'd be able to... Oho, hold on... Yes... That's right...! There's certainly that method...

I descended to the ground and opened up a **[Gate]** to the Regulus Empire. The emperor's palace, to be precise. Suddenly appearing before the king of Hannock wouldn't be smart, so I decided to have the emperor of Regulus introduce me to him.

After hearing that the emperor of Regulus supported me, the king of Hannock accepted my proposal. The Kingdom of Hannock was going to be destroyed and made part of Yulong, so he agreed to my outlandish idea because it was the only way to save his people.

Alrighty, I've got the king's signature... After getting what was needed, I left the castle with the emperor of Regulus.

"Goodness me, you've really gone and done something incredible now…"

"It's just a temporary measure. After I'm sure everyone's safe, I'll get rid of it." The emperor spoke to me in disbelief, shaking his head as he looked over the paperwork.

"Well, Touya. I don't really mind, honestly… I'm just glad this stupid war will end before we have to send even more supplies." I didn't know if it'd go over too smoothly, but there was only one way to find out. I decided to go all-out in my plan.

"What do you mean we don't need to take shelter…?"

"It's fine. I'm going to drive every single Yulong soldier out of Hannock." I showed the king's documentation to Paolo, who had been waiting back at the village for me. He opened his eyes wide in shock as he read it, though I was sure he couldn't quite understand all of it.

"Th-That… A-Are you serious?!"

"Sure am. You can see the king's signature there, yeah? The national seal of Hannock's stamped there, too." Tsubaki peeked over and stared with wide eyes as well.

"I-I'm glad we have the king's approval, but… Well, looking at the way things are going, the country will fall to Yulong soon…" Tsubaki muttered quietly, seemingly not fully understanding the plan. Geez, what a ditz she could be.

"Hey, Tsubaki. Return to the castle and give the following orders to Kousaka and the knight order. While you do that, I'll drive out the Yulong army within Hannock."

"You're going to drive them out…?" I opened up a [Gate] and sent Tsubaki back to Brunhild, completely ignoring the flabbergasted Paolo.

Then, I soared up into the air with [Fly] and blasted off. Within a few moments, I was at Yulong's Capital, Shenhai.

The place looked kind of how I imagined it to look after seeing those masked guys. It was pretty oriental overall. I noticed a huge building which I assumed to be the royal palace. I saw scarlet roof tiles all over the place, and whitewashed walls. Plenty of gold leaf all over as well. Golden sculptures of animals were embedded in pillars, too.

It felt flashy… It was unreasonably bright, like the incarnation of gaudiness itself. It was probably made using people's taxes… If this kind of thing was in Japan, I had no doubt that everyone would hate it. It was just a hunch, but I had a feeling that only the capital looked this nice.

Alright, better go back.

I used a [Gate] to return to the skies above Hannock, surveying the Yulong army there.

"Map. Display. All Yulong military members within Hannock territory."

"Understood. Displaying." With a few little ping noises, the red light on my map showed Yulong's military presence in Hannock.

"[Multiple]. Target Lock."

"Understood. Targets locked." Naturally, my targets were every single Yulong soldier within Hannock.

"Invoke [Gate] beneath the feet of every Yulong soldier."

"Understood. Invoking [Gate]." With that, the red lights signifying Yulong's military presence in Hannock began to fade, bit by bit.

The soldiers of Yulong would at that point begin to appear one after the other inside the royal palace. There you go, heavenly emperor. Enjoy your soldiers.

After making sure every single Yulongese soldier was gone from Hannock, I stepped through a [Gate] and came out at the border between the two nations. The real work was about to begin…

"Wh-What the hell is this?!" I heard a voice from down below. It was no surprise that they were shocked. They'd been warped back to their capital city with no explanation, and then they took the ten-day journey to attempt the invasion again… only to find an enormous wall along the border of Hannock.

Furthermore, the flag atop the wall wasn't Hannock's national elk, but Brunhild's glorious shieldmaiden.

The man on horseback, presumably Yulong's general, yelled up at me. I was standing on the wall next to the flag.

"What is the meaning of this?!"

"Ah, my dear Yulongese soldiers, it's my regretful duty to inform you that your long journey has been wasted. This land here belongs to the Duchy of Brunhild, you see… I can't have anyone crossing it without express permission." I faced the confused army and projected a magnified image of some paperwork for them all to see.

"Wh-What is… No, that can't be…!" It was paperwork approving the transfer of a piece of territory from Hannock to Brunhild. The territory was one kilometer in width along the border of Hannock and Yulong. In other words, the land bordering Yulong was no longer Hannock, but an extension of Brunhild's territory.

So if Yulong's army wanted to invade Hannock, they'd have to pass through Brunhild's land. And we had absolutely no intention of allowing them through.

"Oh, just in case you wanna check, I'll save you the journey. This big old wall spans the entire border." I'd done it. Using the workshop, earth magic, and a mere six days of effort, I'd reconstructed a certain 'great wall' from another world. Well, it was actually a tad higher than the one from Earth.

The wall was about one kilometer wide, all the way down the border line. It was about as wide as the Brunhild territory itself, in fact.

"This is idiotic! We'll just destroy your miserable wall! Charge, men!" At their General's order, the Yulongese soldiers charged on against the wall.

Wow, they're actually doing it… Maybe it's just me, but shouldn't you at least talk with your emperor before declaring war on another country? Well, it's equally possible they don't believe me. I don't really care either way.

The Yulong army approached the wall and began to clamber up it… However, they didn't get far. The moment they started to climb, the ground opened and swallowed them up.

"Whuh?!" The soldiers who made contact with the wall all began to vanish. Everyone behind them stopped marching, seemingly surprised.

I'd set it up so that once the wall was touched, a [Gate] would open up beneath their feet, safely sending them back to Shenghai. Right into the royal palace. Not that I owed them an explanation.

The soldiers took a different approach and began firing arrows up at me. It was all reflected in seconds flat. I'd enchanted the wall with wind magic in such a way that would repel incoming arrows, but would allow outgoing arrows to pass through just fine.

"Oh, here's a little warning. You'd better not unleash any magic spells. Any offensive magic you fire on the wall will be teleported straight to your capital city." I decided to give them a warning since I saw a few mages in the crowd raising their staffs. Upon hearing my words, they lowered their weapons. I didn't know if they believed me, but they sure weren't gonna risk it.

I was telling the truth, though. Any magic on the wall would've gone right through and ended up in Shenghai. Right in the middle of the capital city to boot.

"Now, I'll say it one more time. Go home. Any further acts of aggression will be considered a formal declaration of war." I snapped my fingers and a [Gate] opened in the sky. Ten Chevaliers fell down from the sky, landing just before the wall with a crushing impact. Finally, two black Knight Barons and one white Shining Count descended from the sky as well.

Our Vice-Commanders, Norn and Nikola, were in the Knight Barons, while Lain was riding the Shining Count. The black and white ones were functionally identical, but Shining Count just had a different paint job. I'd painted it a pure and shining white. I figured it'd be better this way, since the commander was supposed to look unique.

"Wh-Wha... No... What?!" The Yulong General fell from his horse, which was bucking and panicking due to the sudden tremors. The horse deserted its master and fled for the hills.

"If you wish to engage us in battle, then the Brunhild knight order will be your foes." At my words, all Frame Gears drew their swords and plunged them into the ground. It was enough for the entire enemy army to completely lose their morale.

"R-Retreat! Get out of here!"

"Get to safety, they'll crush us!"

"Uwaaah!" The entire Yulong army scattered to the winds.

Geez guys, if you wanna get to safety, just touch my wall... You'll be back in Shenghai in seconds, ahahaha!

As I watched the fleeing army, the chest hatch on the black Frame Gear by my side opened. Vice-Commander Norn leaned forward, getting my attention.

"Hey boss... We can definitely defend the land routes like this, but can't they invade Hannock by sea?"

"That'll be fine too. I summoned ten krakens in the seas around Hannock as extra defense. I told them only to attack warships, so it should be fine."

"Wowee... That's pretty mean..." *What do you mean?! It's just basic precaution. At least I don't have to worry about the sky.*

Now all I had to do was check on the state of affairs. I'd laid the bait, so I just had to wait. If the assailants the other day were from Yulong, then they'd definitely use this as a new chance. I expected new movements from their end soon.

All that was left was to apply the finishing touches.

Everything I expected to happen, ended up happening.

We received a formal letter from Yulong. The text was fairly long-winded, but it went like this: "That territory was originally ours, so give it back to us immediately. You have no right to build a wall there. If you do not comply, you will surely be the laughing stock of the world, and your wretched attitude will be exposed. In compensation for the trouble you have caused us so far, we will gladly accept several of your Giant Warriors. The things you call Frame Gears. It's extremely shameless that you use these weapons, as they were originally created by Yulong's forefathers, centuries ago. Have some humility and hand over our rightful technology, you insolent thief."

"They've got some goddamn nerve to say that…"

"They're just attempting to justify themselves. They seem to enjoy twisting stories like that," Kousaka responded with a small shrug and a wry smile. We were both within a guard tower on the Great Wall.

The Great Wall between Yulong and Hannock naturally had a side facing Hannock as well. There weren't any traps or countermeasures on that side, however. The way it was structured was Hannock territory to the west, then the western side of the wall, then Brunhild's territory, then the eastern side of the wall facing Yulong's territory.

I was thinking I'd just give the whole thing to Hannock once the situation died down. I'd give them the Great Wall too.

I didn't really mind because it wasn't like it cost a lot in the grand scheme of things. I would have to remove the traps, though.

"So, what should we send them in response?"

"Eye for an eye, tooth for a tooth. There's no way they could beat us through raw force, but they certainly might try. In the end, I'm their enemy. If it comes down to it, I'll fight against Yulong myself."

"…It's amazing, really… I can't even laugh because I know you're not joking. You'd be a magnificent tyrant, Your Highness." I couldn't deny that I acted selfishly now and then. I didn't even want my own country to begin with… I would've been happy with a simple home with a big garden, honestly. I didn't want to be saddled with national responsibilities.

I wasn't even good at collecting taxes or other stuff like that. The knight order and my maids were paid out of my own pocket, rather than a government wage.

Half of the money I got from Olba I spent on Frame Gear materials, and the other half was more than enough to cover my staff. If I had to describe my knight order, I couldn't call them a national army in that regard. They were kind of more like my personal army.

Still, even if Yulong did wage war with us, they'd really only be marking me as an enemy.

"Tyrant or not, I'm self-aware. Besides, I've been saying this for a while, but... shouldn't you be the grand duke instead of me, Kousaka?"

"I must decline. I honestly believe that if I stay at your side, I can live to see the entire world conquered."

"I don't intend to take over the world, though..."

"That doesn't really matter. Often men find themselves in situations they never intended once it's already come to pass." He had a point. I'd be able to conquer the world fairly easily with the combined power of Babylon and my Frame Gears. But in all honesty, I didn't want to do that. It would've just been me suppressing everyone with overpowering force.

I'd have preferred it if Yulong listened to me and just pulled back.

Someone suddenly knocked at the door. After a few moments, Tsubaki entered the room.

"My liege... We've captured a Yulongese spy."

"One of those masked guys? Good work. Did you get anything out of him?"

"We've been subduing him with some paralyzing poisons that are a bit weaker than your [Paralyze] spell. Flora-dono gave us a truth serum, so we've been interrogating him with that."

What've you been giving them, Flora... I'm sure it'll be fine since it's a Babylon-made medicine, but that's still scary... Apparently they managed to pin him down before he detonated, removed his mask, and used the truth serum on him. He was obviously a spy from Yulong, but I was still squeamish about asking details of his interrogation.

"They're employing various methods to steal the Frame Gears. Plans included assassinating you, kidnapping your fiancees, bribing members of the knight order, and other dubious tactics. It was all approved by Yulong's heavenly emperor."

"Seems we caught them at just the right time, then…" Kousaka muttered quietly. I'd been going easy on them since I had no definitive evidence so far, but now it was different. I had no plans on holding back. I realized that if I didn't do something drastic, they would just keep coming.

"I'd say it's time we became a tad more aggressive, no?"

"Well, I suppose so… If they were planning an assassination, ordinarily that'd be grounds for war. But you don't plan on waging war, do you?" Kousaka looked at me with a knowing grin on his face. It seemed he knew what I was thinking. I was happier than ever to have him serving Brunhild. He was remarkable.

"If we wage a war, the foreign innocents will suffer too. Ideally, I'd want to avoid that. So in this case, I think I should wage a personal war."

"And how do you intend to do that?"

"I want to terrorize their heavenly emperor." I didn't want to cause full-scale panic or actually affect Yulong. Instead, I wanted to show them that I was capable of retaliating with force if they messed with me. I didn't actually want to retaliate, I just wanted to prove a point.

"How, specifically?"

"Well, I was thinking… I could have a knife jabbed in the wall by his bedside, mix something bitter into his food and drink as if to simulate poison, maybe make everyone in the palace vanish for a few hours except for him… Just so he knows that I *could* have him stabbed, poisoned, or spirited away to nowhere, but I'm actively choosing not to."

"G-Goodness me, that's… certainly some extreme harassment."

"…I've heard rumors that this is His Majesty's true nature, Kousaka-sama."

"Psh… It's not that extreme. It'll just make him paranoid, thinking he could be killed any time in any way. The best part is he wouldn't even know if he did die, he'd simply stop existing, so he'd live in constant fear… I'd keep it up until he apologized."

"Well, we shouldn't get into something that extreme right away. For the time being I might suggest that we send a letter back with a tiny implication that suggests we know he's the one responsible for our troubles."

"By the way, what will you do if I get assassinated?"

"I haven't made a plan for that, as I simply don't see it happening."

Tsk, come on now… Don't treat me like I'm immortal! Although, I mean… I guess I might as well be, with all this divinity and stuff. If we're talking about my body, I might slowly actually be turning into a full god or something…

I decided there was no point in worrying about that for the time being.

"Alrighty, then. Send off that letter. It'd be better if we got this matter sorted out as soon as—"

"Milord!" I jumped a little in surprise as Paolo barged into the room. *Don't scare me, damn it!*

"You're feeling rowdy. What's going on?"

"I-I'm s-sorry, Milord! P-Please excuse me, but… there's smoke in the distance, r-rising up on Yulong's side! D-Doesn't that mean the Yulong army is coming in to attack us?!" That didn't sound good, so we rushed up to the top of the guard tower. Looking over Yulong's territory, there were plumes of smoke rising from all over. The carnage was both near and far, on the horizon and more immediately visible too.

"Is it a smoke signal system, or a bushfire…? No, it can't be that…" There was no way a bushfire could be that widespread. I had no idea what was going on, but there was chaos erupting everywhere. Fire and smoke dotted the scenery.

"Wh-What… What's that in the distance? It's… glimmering?"

Glimmering? What's he talking about? I narrowed my eyes, looking over at what Paolo pointed out. It definitely looked like something shiny… Though as it came closer, I noticed it was more reflecting the light than shining itself.

Seconds later, the truth clicked in my mind. I was already screaming.

"G-Get in the Frame Gears, now! Action stations, people! We have an incoming assault!" I immediately invoked [Fly] to soar over there and confirm the reality of this nightmare.

"Ghah… Wh-What the hell kind of timing is this?!" A roaring crowd of Phrase were charging toward my wall.

There were various shapes and sizes, several small and medium-sized ones, with a few larger ones as well. The majority of them were Lesser Constructs, but there were a few Intermediate Constructs in the mix. Some were shaped like ants, some like centipedes, others had funnier shapes, like that of an ostrich. Overall, there were ten Phrase lifeforms larger than my standard Frame Gears.

They weren't running especially fast. However, that wasn't the problem. The problem was that there were around one-hundred of them.

"Target Lock! Phrase Cores! Invoke [**Apport**] now!"

"Understood. Invoking [**Apport**]." A large Phrase Core around the side of a softball appeared in my hand.

Shit, this is bad... I can't pull out more than one at a time, since the spell's limited to whatever I can fit in my palm. Pulling them out one-by-one is gonna take too much time, and I'll only be able to kill the small ones this way! What do I do?!

"Entwine thus, Earth! Cursed Soil: [Earthbind]!" Tree roots burst from the ground and snared the legs of the incoming Phrase. Just as I thought that would buy us a little time, the creatures easily broke free.

They'd sliced their own legs off... They could regenerate them instantly, so they simply discarded them and advanced. The Phrase were truly monstrous in their actions.

From behind me, Lain arrived in her Shining Count, and Nikola showed up in his Knight Baron. A few Chevaliers appeared alongside them, too. They'd left a few units behind to protect the wall.

I flew to the side of the white knight and relayed orders to Lain.

"Take out the larger ones while I destroy the smaller ones! They can regenerate, so focus on the core inside their body! Make sure everyone on the comms channel gets that info!"

"Roger!" Lain replied through the speakers. Satisfied she understood, I moved to take my Phrase Greatsword out of [**Storage**]. It was about two meters long and thirty centimeters wide. I hefted it in both hands.

If I hadn't applied [**Gravity**] to reduce the weight of it, there was no way in hell I would've been able to lift it.

"Charge!" I barreled toward a group of nearby Phrase. I aimed straight for the core of my first target, and was able to split it in two with little resistance. My sword was sharper than it had any right to be due to all the magic energy I'd poured into it, of course.

In a similar fashion, I began to cut down more of them, one by one. I dipped and dived between their extending, sharpened crystalline tentacles, and got a good glance at an enormous Intermediate Construct facing off against a few heavy knights.

They lunged forward, shields raised to defend against lance-like limbs, battering away at it with their weapons.

But the Frame Gears I'd stationed at the wall were not equipped with specialized weaponry, so they were having a tough time of it. The broken pieces of the Phrase just kept regenerating, so they had to constantly attack in quick succession to make any of their hits matter.

Only Nikola in his Knight Baron had anything special. It was a halberd. He was fighting solo against another Intermediate and actually managed to shatter its core. Then, he immediately went to support the struggling Chevaliers nearby.

There were about ten Intermediate Constructs. We had five Chevaliers, one Knight Baron, and one Shining Count. I wondered if it'd be enough. One of the heavy knights that Nikola rushed to aid managed to shatter an Intermediate core. Working in tandem definitely had its perks. That knight then went on to support another struggling knight, and Nikola turned to support another of his comrades as well.

And that was when I realized our advantage. The Phrase were not coordinated creatures. From a Phrase's perspective, each battle was a solo battle. If another of their kind nearby was in trouble, they wouldn't rush to support them. That was the point where we had a clear advantage. I decided to entrust the Intermediate Constructs to the knights in the Frame Gears. There were close to nine times as many Lesser Constructs, after all, and I needed to wipe them out fast.

I sliced through the Phrase like butter, one by one.

And then, by a strange stroke of luck, if you wanted to call it that, the Phrase finally stopped charging toward the wall. They stopped and turned to me, seemingly recognizing me as an enemy.

The fact that Phrase operated in such a rigid, mechanical manner could be considered a weak point. They operated on basic instinct, so you could say they were easier to guide in the heat of battle... but it also made them deadlier, and efficient. The threats I'd issued to Yulong the other day wouldn't work on an enemy like this. The Phrase knew no fear. Instead, they just advanced onward without feeling. They were like harvesters, terminators.

There was certainly no time for me to rest, either. Most of the attacks were from their spear-like limbs, but now there were some of those crystal missiles coming at me, much like that time I faced off against the Manta Phrase. I defended against it with [Shield] and took out the one responsible.

"G-Geez... Fighting this many at once is nuts..." The enemies were acting so disorderly, too. There was no method to their madness. I couldn't invoke something like [Ice Rock] or [Gate] since they needed to stay in place. [Paralyze] and [Gravity] were ineffective, as well. I couldn't use [Slip] for fear of affecting my allies either.

I briefly considered using [Gravity] to make my allies' swords heavier, but it would've been too much to explain in the heat of the moment.

All I could do was kill, kill, and kill some more. Until eventually...

"...Alright, that's it!" Around ten minutes later... or maybe even less than ten minutes later, there were no more Lesser Constructs remaining.

Lain killed the final Intermediate Construct around the same time. At least, it looked like she'd killed it.

I didn't see the moment she crushed the core, so I kept my guard up for another ten minutes. That time passed by without any movement from the broken fragments all over the place, so it looked like it was really over.

There wasn't too much damage to our side. Two Frame Gears had broken blades, and one had a shattered shield, but the rest had minor scuffs and scrapes all over the Frames. I knew Rosetta would cry upon seeing it, either way.

"Milord... Just what were those things?" Lain opened up the white knight's chest hatch and spoke to me. It actually reminded me that I hadn't explained anything about the Phrase to the knight order yet. I invoked [Fly] and hopped up to the Shining Count's shoulder.

"They're called the Phrase. They're invaders from another world. They once destroyed civilization during ancient times... The Frame Gears you're piloting were originally weapons designed to combat them." Calling them invaders wasn't quite right, in all honesty. They were more like exterminators. And we were the vermin that they so viciously sought out.

This is the first time I've seen so many at once... I don't even want to think about what might've happened if Hannock hadn't given me this plot of land.

"Then… does that mean the smoke plumes we saw earlier were caused by these guys? Were they attacking Yulong villages or something?"

"That's possible, yeah… Oh… Shit, wait! All troops, move back! We're in Yulong's territory right now, as a full fighting force! We can't risk being sighted by their intelligence corps or anything like that!" It was entirely possible they'd blame all the destruction on us.

I was about to collect the Phrase fragments, but hesitated and only ended up taking about half. It would've been suspicious if all the evidence of Phrase activity here was erased. At least leaving half meant the Yulong government would have to accept we weren't the attackers here.

"Politics really is a pain in the ass sometimes…" As I grumbled about the state of the situation, I pulled up the map on my phone. I had it display places with rising smoke and recent destruction. As I'd expected, there were a few places in the area. The Phrase must've done it.

Unfortunate as it was, there didn't seem to be any survivors. Phrase could hear the beats of a human heart, after all. Hiding did nothing, since they could track you no matter what.

As I quietly lamented the dead, I zoomed the map out until the entirety of Yulong had become visible.

"Hold on… What's… What's going on here…?" *Aren't there a little too many damaged markers? Why's there smoke rising up in the south? That's way away from here… W-Wait, Shenghai too? What's going on? N-No, it can't be…*

"Run search. Display Phrase."

"Understood. Displaying."

Thud. A pin fell down on the map, indicating the presence of a Phrase.

Thud. Another fell. *Thud. Thud. Thud. Thud. Thud. Thudthudth udthudthudthudthudthudthudthudthudthud.*

Thudthudthudthudthudthudthudthudthudthudthudthud.
Thudthudthudthudthudthudthudthudthudthudthudthud.
Thudthudthudthudthudthudthudthudthudthudthudthud.
Thudthudthudthudthudthudthudthudthudthudthudthud.
Thudthudthudthudthudthudthudthudthudthudthudthud.
Thudthudthudthudthudthudthudthudthudthudthudthud.
Thudthudthudthudthudthudthudthudthudthudthudthud.
Thudthudthudthudthudthudthudthudthudthudthudthud.

Countless red pointers fell down upon Yulong, almost obscuring the country itself.

"No way…" I could only watch on in horror, letting out a small gasp as the pins kept falling.

I briefly lost my composure and didn't know what to do. The pins kept dropping until the entire map was almost completely covered.

"…How many Phrase in total?"

"Thirteen-thousand-one-hundred-and-sixty-nine   Phrase lifeforms in total." That number was simply unfathomable. I had no idea how to respond to that. Defeating them could be possible, but it would take a long time. And each minute I wasted, more of Yulong's citizens would die. It was none of my business… I just had to reinforce the idea that it had nothing to do with me… But I couldn't.

"Gh… Wh-What the hell do I do?!"

"Ah, Touya… Just as I'd expected." I turned around in shock at the sudden voice, only to find myself faced with a pale young man.

"Ende?!"

"Yeah… A lot of the 'noise' I'd been hearing from Phrase cores was being snuffed out in this area… I was looking for the cause, and… It seems like I've found it, hm?" With a huge smile on his face, Ende walked my way. He was clad in his usual outfit, complete with his white scarf. He looked at the Shining Count behind me with very curious eyes.

"Now that's something special… Are these of your design, Touya? Would you mind if I rode around in one?"

"Ah, well… I didn't really make them or anything, but… Hey wait, more importantly than that… there are Phrase everywhere! Do you know what happened?!"

"Yes, I do… You do too. The boundary's torn."

The dimensional boundary. The invisible fabric that separated this world from others. The unthinkable had happened. The Phrase had ripped it apart and poured through.

"Wait, you're saying the boundary's gone?!"

"Mm… Not exactly. This particular incident is an accidental occurrence. The Phrase in this country simply 'fell' through an area where the fabric was particularly thin. The boundary isn't torn all over, it's just strained."

Oh, wow… That means if we can take care of the ones here I can rest easy a little longer… I don't even know if I can take care of them all, but… It's not like I really have a choice, is it?

"Is there a way to kill them all fast? Or all at once?"

"Hm… I wouldn't say it's possible to kill them all at the same time. That being said, we could definitely draw their attention…"

"How?!"

"We could draw them here with the Sovereign's voice."

The Sovereign's voice...? What does the Sovereign Phrase have to do with this?

"Phrase cores produce noise. Each operates on a unique and distinct wavelength, and the Sovereign Core is no exception to this rule. The Sovereign Core currently exists within a living creature in this world, so its noise is obscured by the heartbeat of its host. So... what if we were to emit the 'noise' of the Sovereign Core right here?"

"All the Phrase in the area would come this way..."

"Bingo." It seemed like a sound plan in practice, but I was amazed Ende had such a method.

Luring them here with a fake noise is one thing, but... can we really take on over ten-thousand of these things without serious casualties?

Well, if I think about it this way, they'll all be in various villages and towns... Places where humans are. We won't have to fight all of them at the same time, since they'll come here in staggered formation. But if we can't beat them fast enough, the numbers will just pile up...

"Can you really bring them here?"

"I can. I have an item that has the Sovereign's wavelength sealed within it. Within the wavelength is the 'noise,' which is indistinguishable from the real thing." Ende suddenly pulled out a long, thin glass slide. He held it between his index and middle finger. It looked like a slide used on a microscope, or for storing scientific specimens.

"This is one of my personal storage devices. I can keep various things inside them. Using them, I can preserve things from large living specimens to noises. If I open this, the Sovereign's noise will ring out, so the nearby Phrase will hear it and charge toward us."

Wow, that's pretty damn impressive... Well, he's wily, I'll give him that, but... What's with this guy? I don't get his angle at all. He can't be called an ally of the Phrase, but still...

I reached my hand toward the slide he held out, but moments before I touched it, he pulled his hand back.

Wait, what? You're not sharing?

"But... I don't think I want to." Ende grinned wide as he spoke.

What the hell are you playing at...

"Why?"

"I want that." He pointed to the Frame Gear.

What... Ghh... What the hell? You're getting all googly-eyed over a Frame Gear at a time like this? What are you, a kid?!

"...Do you promise not to use it for anything weird?"

"I totally promise! Have a little faith in me." It wouldn't be possible for him to use the Frame Gear against us, since there were emergency protocols and all to prevent that. I couldn't understand his motives at all, but he seemed to have a personal vendetta against the Phrase. I didn't really think he was fully on our side, but I could hardly consider him an enemy, either. Even so, I wasn't sure if it'd be smart or not to hand a Frame Gear over to him. But if I didn't give him one, he wouldn't give me the Sovereign's noise slide. I was in a predicament I never thought I'd be in to begin with. But I knew I needed him to come out on top in this situation, so I was out of options. I decided to add in a caveat, at least a small victory.

"If it's stolen, given away, or sold to a foreign nation, I wouldn't appreciate it..."

"I won't sell it, or hand it over, or let it get stolen, promise! Please, please, lemme have it. I'll treat it right. I'm begging you, Touyaaa... Look, I'll kill all the Phrase around here too, okay? How about it?"

What's with this guy? He's acting like he's just gonna hop in and have full control. Then again, knowing this guy's overpowered nonsense, I guess he probably could... He's way abnormal by this world's standards... I actually find him a little obnoxious... Damn him to hell, how come he's better than me?!

I've met him a few times, and I don't think he's a bad guy... That's just my intuition, though... If only Yumina was here!

His offer of helping me fight the Phrase was tempting... After all, I knew it would save me a lot of time and effort.

I invoked [Gate] and summoned the Red Dragon Knight, Dragoon, from the hangar.

"Here, it's a Frame Gear with a focus on mobility. I call it the Dragoon."

"Whoa! It's red! That's, like, super cool." The Frame Gear I'd chosen was one that was particularly hard to control. I decided to just push it onto Ende because nobody but me could handle it anyway.

Ende lazily tossed the slide over to me and climbed up onto the Dragon Knight. The hatch opened up and he clambered on in.

He started it up immediately and the Frame began to walk around. After a while he had it running, and moving its arms with surprising dexterity. Then, he deployed the wheels and moved as gracefully as he could in its high-mobility mode.

Wh-What the hell... Why's he better with it than me?

"Oh, this is pretty simple to maneuver. I like it."

"...Hah, yeah... G-Good for you." I reluctantly answered Ende with stiffest smile I could muster. That bastard had no business being more overpowered than me.

"But, uh, doesn't it have any weapons?"

"Oh... Right, I forgot to prepare any." The Dragon Knight didn't have a lot of power, so it couldn't really handle heavy weaponry. I had intended to make a lightweight weapon for it from Phrase fragments, but never got around to the actual deed.

Luckily for me there was a veritable mountain of dead Phrase nearby.

I used [**Modeling**] to craft two shortswords from some fallen Phrase appendages. Then, I made two sheaths, and fitted them onto the Dragoon's back.

"Alrighty! I'll go kill a bunch of Phrase, just as agreed."

"Hey, wait! Before you go anywhere, tell me how to use this thing!" I hurriedly waved the slide at Ende.

"Oh, right. Just smash it and the sound should echo out. You can't copy the noise through technology or magic, so don't go getting any ideas."

Oh, really...? Well, there goes my plan of recording it on my smartphone.

As I lamented my ruined plan, Ende took another two slides and tossed them at me.

"Here, these two are identical. If you use them all at the same time in different places, you can scatter the Phrase to your advantage." Ende clambered back into the Dragoon and sped off. The guy was an efficient Phrase-killer, so I was sure he'd do well. I'd prefer him to just kill all of them, though...

His Frame Gear was red, so it gave off a pretty powerful vibe. *Heh... It'd be funny if he came back wearing a mask next time...*

Enough of that... Don't have time to think stupid thoughts! I've got plenty to do, after all.

I returned to the Brunhild castle and explained everything to the people there. The situation in Yulong, the Phrase, the dimensional boundary, and why I had the Frame Gears to begin with... I came clean about it all.

"...The scale of our conversation just became... considerably larger..." Old man Yamagata breathed out heavily after I spoke. Baba, standing next to him, folded his arms with a soft frown on his face.

"I understand if you don't believe me, but..."

"No, I've no reason to doubt you. Creatures from another world... Surely if we do nothing, then the tragedy of the ancient kingdom will befall us as well." Kousaka readily believed me, but that was probably because he saw all the smoke back in Yulong.

"Putting that aside for now, we need to figure out the situation fully. The priority would be the current invasion of Yulong. Your Highness... Do you want to save their citizens?"

"If I can, yes. We're the only ones who can oppose the Phrase."

"You shouldn't." Kousaka immediately shot down my idea. He basically spoke words that would sentence Yulong's people to death. They didn't have any method to oppose the Phrase. If they pulled out all the stops of their military might, maybe they'd do okay, but there was no way they could survive such a horde through conventional means.

"I will readily fight if my country is under attack. However, I see no need to risk life and limb for a country that is not only unfriendly with us, but actively hostile."

"But... if it keeps up like this, the casualties won't stop at Yulong alone. This isn't a situation where you can just worry about a certain nation's attitude. People are dying even as we speak. Are you saying we shouldn't help them?"

"Your Highness... You are a tremendous man with an equally tremendous heart. But you can't just..."

"Kousaka, listen up." Baba, who had been quiet up until this point, finally spoke up.

"We know more'n anyone about what our leader is like, aye? Didn't he help us, despite Takeda being his enemy back then?"

"I... But... the situation is different now. He has an entire country on his shoulders."

"An' that's where yer wrong. He ain't burdened. I climbed up onto his shoulders at my own leisure. If he shakes me off, then I fall off. If I don't like it, then I can climb off. Didn't we come here to see where the wind would blow?"

"...That we did." Kousaka exhaled quietly as he spoke. He was likely just nervous, so I knew I wouldn't hold his pragmatic speech against him.

"Given the course of action you desire, even if I disagree, we should make our move soon. But if we are to intervene, you should inform the western alliance first. We must formally let them know our intent." He was right about that, at least. I had no idea just what the ramifications of this invasion would be on the global stage. It was important to get the whole thing ironed out before I made my move, though I couldn't afford to waste any time.

I was in a rush, after all. People were being systematically slaughtered one after the other as I played politics. Ordinarily I'd send the other monarchs letters, but I decided to appeal directly to them at their homes. I needed to hurry, and they needed to learn the truth immediately.

"I see... The Phrase, hm... If those fiends are truly our enemies, then I see no problem with you creating those Frame Gears, Touya." The king of Belfast leaned back in his chair, which lightly creaked. *Well, it's not like I invented them or anything...*

I was in a meeting with the leaders of the western alliance. The king of Belfast, the emperor of Regulus, the emperor of Refreese, the beastking of Mismede, the pope of Ramissh, and the newly-crowned king of Lihnea. There were six national representatives in total present.

First, I explained everything about the Phrase to the gathered rulers. That they were invaders from another world that had appeared long ago to destroy the world. Then, I explained the current situation in Yulong. I did not tell them about the Sovereign Phrase or Babylon, however. I tweaked the story to one about me discovering the Frame Gear in some ancient ruins, learning how to repair one, and then replicating the process to manufacture more. It wasn't strictly a lie, all things considered. I just felt they didn't need to know everything.

"These... Phrase, was it? Are they all that strong?"

"They've appeared in my country before, lad. Well, just one of them... From what I heard, magic didn't affect it, it could regenerate, and its skin was tougher than old boots!" The beastking of Mismede answered King Cloud. He must've been talking about the Snake Phrase that Leen took care of some time ago.

"But still, for ten-thousand, or rather, more than that... to come out in Yulong... Touya, is this a special case? Or are we to fear this happening again in the future?"

"This is a very rare set of circumstances, I assure you. That being said, they still may appear now and then, but not nearly as many as this. Still, I do need to be honest with you all. There is the possibility of a massive invasion occurring sometime in the future. As to when or where they'd come through, I cannot say."

"Goodness me... I-I suppose we shouldn't worry about such things for now, though." The emperor of Regulus quickly quieted down. I was hardly what you could call a Phrase specialist, but I was probably the only person in the world other than Ende who knew much about them.

"To be honest, it's possible they may start appearing in your countries too. For that reason, I'd like you to take a look at this." I projected a video onto the wall of the conference room. It was a video I had a summoned bird record as it flew across Yulong's skies.

The video, taken from a very high vantage point, clearly showed a massive army of Phrase annihilating a village. They hunted down every human without end, mercilessly slaughtering them with incredible precision and efficiency. The six leaders had their eyes trained on the video, watching in horror as sweat beaded upon their brows.

"So these are the Phrase…"

"Yes. This video isn't a live broadcast, so it's not happening right now or anything. This particular incident happened about an hour ago. After the Phrase destroyed this village, they continued their march and proceeded to kill everyone in the neighboring village." After the bird had returned my smartphone, and I'd seen the video, I felt absolutely hopeless. I'd initially intended just to get some shots of the Phrase, so I didn't think we'd actually catch an attack in progress. My heart ached to think about how they could've been saved, but I knew I needed to show it to the rulers of the western alliance. They had to understand what they were up against.

I wanted them to understand just how dire the situation was. I also wanted them to imagine this happening in their own nations.

"What of Shenghai, Yulong's capital?" In response to the emperor of Refreese's question, I stopped the video and pulled up the map. The red lights that represented the Phrase were crawling around Yulong. They were likely following their instincts and heading toward towns and villages in order to kill every human being in the area.

Shenghai was completely dyed in red.

"There's some resistance going on, but it's only a matter of time before they all die. The Phrase have one purpose here. Our extermination. They won't leave Shenghai until everyone in the capital city is dead."

"God save us…" The pope cupped her hands over her mouth, clearly horrified. The Phrase moved like machines operating solely to hunt and kill humans. They massacred everyone in one area, and then immediately locked on to the next signal. They were like locusts hopping from crop to crop, devastating the harvest in their senseless hunger.

"Touya… Over here… in southern Shenghai, are the Phrase not vanishing one by one?"

"Huh?" Lihnea's king pointed out an area on the map where the red lights were rapidly going out. *Huh, what could… Oh! That's Ende!*

"That's the result of someone currently working with me. I granted him a Frame Gear for personal use. What you're most likely seeing here are the fruits of his labor."

"Oh, I see. It's certainly killing them at great speed… Well, this definitely shows the efficiency of your weapon." Ende was probably strong enough to kill them alone, but that was a different matter entirely. We needed to focus on the extermination of the Phrase. As if to briskly change the subject, I clapped my hands together.

"Brunhild will engage the Phrase in Yulong using our Frame Gears. As leaders of the western alliance, I'd like to ask for your approval."

"Wh-What?! Wait a minute... Are you saying you plan on opposing those things?" I'd caught the beastking by surprise. That was slightly amusing, but understandable. Even if I made use of every single person in Brunhild who could pilot a Frame Gear, like the knight order, and Yumina along with the other girls, it would only be around one-hundred fighters on the field. In that case we'd be able to win if each pilot took down around one-hundred Phrase, but it was still a senseless course of action.

"The Frame Gears have an emergency eject magic in case of serious damage. The magic sends the pilot off to safety. It can do this if it detects the cockpit being crushed, pierced, or damaged and so on... However, in the case of instant death scenarios, it might not have time to activate." Thanks to the mass-production I had going on, we had a lot of Frame Gears to spare. In the worst-case scenario we simply had to perform a lot of repairs one-by-one.

The pope suddenly raised her hand, looking right at me.

"Touya... I have a question. In regards to our dear old friend... Are the Phrase His enemies as well?"

"...I'm not sure if they're His enemies or not. He told me that He didn't know much about them. But our dear old friend won't be interfering with what happens here. The Phrase are our problem, not His."

"What are you two going on about?" The emperor of Refreese tilted his head in bemusement. He couldn't understand what we were talking about. That was only natural, since our dear old friend was God Almighty after all.

"Very well, then. The Theocracy of Ramissh stands with Brunhild. Many of our Knights Templar have made use of the Frame Unit simulation you loaned to us, Touya. Our nation can spare a few capable pilots."

"Huh?" *Huh, so the templars are helping me as well? That's actually a great relief… I hope they understand what they're getting into, though.* Seeing the pope's brazen proclamation, the beastking suddenly raised his hand.

"Hey now, Mismede also offers its support to Brunhild! I definitely can't leave a situation as interesting as this one alone."

"Belfast will naturally participate as well."

"And Regulus."

"Refreese, as well."

"L-Lihnea stands with Brunhild, too!"

"Uhm… Are you all sure? This situation's pretty dangerous, you know…" Just as I was about to explain the dangers again, they all drowned me out with protests that basically amounted to "We've made our decision, deal with it." These guys were a real handful.

Still, the mission was basically all risk for no benefit. I couldn't understand why they'd join. When I mentioned that detail, the king of Belfast spoke up.

"We have our reasons, believe me. To begin with, Yulong's national power will decrease after this, so they're going to need to rely on foreign aid. It's better to curry favor with them now to put them in our debt. Secondly, we would like our own knights to gain experience in combat against the Phrase. We know not when or if our nations might end up in the same situation as Yulong. Third, we wish to make sure Brunhild is protected. Or more specifically, you. The products and culture of your nation are a treasured thing, my boy. If you were to die during this incident, we'd lose a revolutionary figure. That's how I see it, at least."

That made sense. It was a pretty cunning way of operating. Even if Yulong survived this, we had no idea what would happen afterward. And we had no idea if the heavenly emperor was still alive, either.

I personally didn't care if the heavenly emperor was dead or not. Probably because he'd tried to kill me. I just wanted to help the people of Yulong.

"The issue is the situation that'll develop after this is over…"

"Do you think the neighboring countries might invade the weakened Yulong?"

"Would they? If that happens, then the Brunhild territory at Hannock's border might come in handy." *Let's see… Currently, the nations bordering Yulong are… One, two, three… Six. If Eashen enters the situation, then that's seven potential risks.*

To the west was the Kingdom of Hannock. To the north was Xenoahs, the Demon Kingdom. The Nokia Kingdom was to the north-east, and Eashen, the Divine Nation, was over the sea to the east as well. The Horn Kingdom and the Kingdom of Felsen were to the south. Then across a river, the Roadmare Union was to the south-west.

It was almost impossible to predict what would happen to such a massive country with so many elements surrounding them.

For now, we decided to deal with the matter at hand.

"Since you're all cooperating with me, I'll send you twenty Frame Gears each. Eighteen Heavy Knights, and two Black Knights for your commanders. Please take care in selecting your pilots. There'll be around ninety Frame Gears from Brunhild, and one-hundred-and-twenty from the other allied nations. We'll face them down with a combined force of around two-hundred-and-ten."

"Our numbers pale in comparison… I suppose each soldier will have to kill around fifty of them to even out the odds. Honestly, I doubt our chances, but… Do you perhaps have a plan?"

"At present, the Phrase types making up the invasion are Lesser Constructs and Intermediate Constructs. The Lesser Constructs should be a piece of cake if we use the Frame Gears properly. Run search. Display Intermediate Constructs. Denote with blue markers." Suddenly, several red lights on the map changed into blue ones.

"Beginning search. Search complete. Displaying. Total Intermediate Constructs: One-thousand-and-thirty-five."

"…So, about ten percent of them. Even if each person takes down five of them, we should be alright. We might be able to manage it, after all…" The emperor of Refreese muttered, glaring at the screen and patting the top of his shiny bald head.

"Well, in theory… But in practice there'll be a lot of Lesser Constructs around, so it'll be a bit more complicated to take them on. I do have a plan, though." I began introducing my strategy. It wasn't an especially complex one, either. The plan was to use the Sovereign noise I'd received from Ende to have the Phrase split and travel in three directions.

Then, I would actively use my [Gate] magic to send fighters around the battlefield as they're needed. We simply had to balance our units and deploy them to the relevant areas at the right times.

"Ah, wait a moment… Does that mean you won't be piloting a Frame Gear, Touya?"

"That's right, yes. I'll be using my flight magic to soar high above the battlefield. I'll provide support and basically be your backup unit." I answered the pope's inquiry confidently. Having me as support was probably the wisest choice. There was no telling what kind of unexpected trouble could pop up out of the blue. I had to be in a position to move freely and respond to danger.

"Indeed, that's only sensible. In a battlefield divided in three, only Touya can see the full scope of the field. And only he can send people to and fro using his magic."

"That's right. Plus, I have combat capabilities to oppose the Phrase hand-to-hand."

"Hrmph… But if you can fight them without a Frame Gear… why bother having one in the first place?"

"It's true that I can take them down as I am, but it takes time. More time than it should. If I pilot a Frame Gear, I can smash them freely." I answered the emperor of Refreese's inquiry and hurriedly ended the meeting before more stupid questions popped up. Yulong was in the midst of crisis, so I had no more time for chitchat. We needed to hurry.

"I'll gather you all in one hour. Use this time to pick out your pilots and explain the situation."

I opened up a [Gate] and sent the leaders, along with their escorts, back home.

We had a lot to do. A lot to do and not nearly enough time. We had to hurry.

"Oh gosh… Something bad happened and I didn't even notice, huh…?" The god of love… Or, uh, Karen, my sister… munched on a cookie as she heard me explain everything. …*You're getting crumbs all over the carpet.*

"Yeah… So… I was wondering if you'd be able to help us out."

"Ohh… No can do, little bro. My powers are free-to-use if it's a love-related matter. But I can't do anything unrelated to love unless it's to do with catching that servile god, y'know?"

"Love-related matters… Like what, exactly?"

"Hmhm… I mean something like… bringing a boy knight and a girl knight together on the battlefield. And splitting them up, all the same…"

Kind of useless… Lovey-dovey matters won't mean anything against the Phrase. Guess it was pointless asking her for help.

"You were thinking something impolite just now, weren'tcha?"

"Owh… Sh-Shorry! Lemmeh goh… Thaht hurhts!" I sputtered out a frantic apology as Karen pinched my cheek.

Damn it, even this god's a bully…! She sits here casually and only gets serious for stupid stuff!

"…You thought something rude again, y'know?"

"E-Excuhse me! Owh! Owwwh!!!" I could tolerate the pinching because I was, well, me. But if she did that to a regular person they'd have probably died… She was a truly terrifying force. I rubbed my pained face as I shuffled off to Babylon.

Rosetta, Monica, and the mini-bots were in the middle of applying some last-minute adjustments to some Frame Gears.

"What's going on?"

"Well, we've somehow managed to make a go at it… There's two-hundred-and-ten Frame Gears here, sir! We have forty spare units, making two-hundred-and-fifty in total, yessir! They'll be ready to deploy in thirty minutes on the dot!"

"Master… You should, like, totally take me to the battlefield and stuff… I will show those Phrase a monstrous death unlike any they have known thus far!" Monica yelled loudly as she hefted her wrench over her shoulder. It was undeniable that out of all the Babylon Gynoids, she was the most attuned to combat. I actually wanted her to focus on maintenance though, so we didn't have the luxury to send her out like that.

"Do you see the details I've added here, sir?! The pauldrons are a different color depending on the nation! I've also added the royal crest of each country to the respective Frame Gears, sir!"

"Good work." The right shoulders of each Frame Gear were painted in different colors depending on the nation they were assigned to. Belfast was red, Refreese was blue, Regulus was purple, Mismede was green, Ramissh was yellow, and Lihnea was orange. The left shoulders were also painted, but had numbers denoting which unit they were. It didn't exactly look too aesthetically pleasing, but it was necessary to tell who was who on the battlefield.

It was a quick job though, so it wasn't like we could do much to prevent it.

"What about weapons?"

"They're being manufactured in the workshop, sir! But the amount of Phrase weapons is limited!"

"Well, I guess we're lacking materials… Still, can't the workshop make weapons for the Frame Gear out of smaller chunks?"

"Master, sir! The workshop isn't quite like your **[Modeling]** spell! We can't just slap small fragments of Phrase together to make big stuff! Making small weapons for humans is fine and all, but making Frame Gear sized stuff en masse is inefficient and largely wasteful, sir!"

"To like, use an example and stuff… mass-producing stuff in the workshop is, like, uhm… using a dagger as a replacement for a spear tip. It's quite fine for mass-producing arrowheads and such, but you still have to aim properly to get them to work. The weaponry you'll produce here may end up hindering your men rather than helping them. Plus, like, without your magic pouring into them, the stuff's all brittle and dumb…!" I got the picture, at any rate. Without my magic going into them, phrasium weaponry was as good as glass.

71

The Frame Gears and their weapons all seemed sorted. Now all I had to do was look over the knight order.

I didn't even make it to the barracks before they all came anxiously running toward me.

"Milord… We're done preparing. We can deploy at any time." Rebecca spoke up confidently. Logan, who was standing next to her, also nodded firmly. Neither displayed even a hint of fear.

Not every member of the knight order would be boarding Frame Gears and joining the fight. Certain demonkin, like ogres and lamias, couldn't board them, for example. Plus, a few members of the knight order simply couldn't ride Frame Gears due to claustrophobia, motion sickness, and other various reasons.

Those members would stay at the base and offer support in whatever ways they could.

"That's good. Listen, don't worry. Also, don't try to be a hero. Your lives are the most important things here. If you think you're in danger, there's no shame in fleeing. There's no honor in dying to one of those, I promise you. Once we all get home safely, we'll celebrate, okay?" I found myself speaking to them all, reminding them that they were important. I didn't want a single one of them to lose hope. I didn't want a single one of them to die.

"Don't overestimate your own capabilities. You must never make light of your foes, either. There's no shame in a little bit of fear. If one isn't enough, then make use of the power of two. If that's still no good, then three. You cannot afford to fight these monsters fairly." I planned to support them as much as I could, but there'd naturally be times I couldn't be there. The Frame Gears had an emergency escape option, at the very least. Still, if the cockpit were crushed, there wouldn't be any saving them.

Safety was the number one priority. After reminding them of that, I returned to the castle.

I went to the den and found Elze and the others waiting for me. I asked Elze and Yae to join me in battle. The other three would wait on standby at base and help out those that wound up injured.

"B-But... I can fight, I really can...!"

"Lu, you're the princess of Regulus. We can't have you fighting alongside Regulus' knight order. They may prioritize your safety over the mission." It was mostly the same in Yumina's case, as well. As for Linze, she wasn't exactly suited for this kind of combat. The Phrase could absorb magic, and we needed her Light spells to heal any potentially injured people.

"Elze, Yae, and Lain will be deployed at three different key locations. Also, I'm going to have Kokuyou and Sango join Elze, Kohaku join Yae, and Kougyoku join Lain. That way they'll be able to stay in contact with me." Thanks to telepathy, we could talk no matter the distance. Information like that would be vital for me to know how to move around the battlefield.

"Touya, please don't overdo it..."

"It'll be okay. We'll all come back safely. It's getting close to the time, though... We need to head out." I took everyone with me through a **[Gate]**. We came out at my wall on Hannock's border, at a special facility I had come to call... HQ.

Right on the border of Hannock stood the Great Wall of Brunhild. In front of it stood around two-hundred-and-fifty Frame Gears. The view was incredible.

Each country's knights had boarded their vehicles and were waiting to mobilize. At the HQ, the rulers of each country were observing Phrase activity on a large projected board made of several screens.

There were sixteen different screens and feeds, lined up in a four by four set of rows and columns. Each one displayed different images and video feeds.

I'd summoned several Valkyries earlier and asked them to fly around with cameras to record the situation properly.

"I'm glad we're here. This way we can see the state of affairs."

"...The anticipation is killing me, I must admit." I stood next to the pope of Ramissh, and the emperor of Refreese. I looked around the room a bit, then addressed the Commanders and Vice-Commanders of each nation.

Belfast's officers were Commander Neil and Vice-Commander Lyon. Regulus' commander was the old, one-eyed Gaspar, and Mismede's Vice-Commander was the wolf beastman, Garm. I only knew those four.

I vaguely recognized the other commanders and vice-commanders, but I'd never exchanged words with them.

"Alright, so here's the general idea. Ninety Frame Gears from Brunhild will divide into three teams of thirty. Then, they'll deploy at three separate locations that are on opposite sides of the capital of Yulong. I've tentatively named these squads A, B, and C. Belfast and Regulus will accompany A Squad, Mismede and Ramissh will accompany B Squad, and Refreese and Lihnea will accompany C Squad. This creates three teams of seventy members, and all you need to do after deploying is wait for my command." I displayed three markers on the projected map, indicating points A, B, and C.

"The Phrase should begin moving toward point A when I begin the plan. After attracting the main group there, I'll move to point B and attract a splinter group of them to that location. Then, I'll move to point C and perform the same action, effectively thinning them out into three manageable groups." Lyon tentatively raised his hand.

"And if they don't split up evenly?"

"I'll be able to use **[Gate]** to freely send units between points. Ideally, I'll move ten units at a time as a single team, but I'd prefer for countries not to get too jumbled up."

"And how might we communicate?"

"Each Frame Gear has a short-range communication device. The range isn't too big, so you won't be able to communicate with people at other points, but you can freely talk to other people in your vicinity. As for long-range comms… That's where these three come in. Yae, Elze, and Lain can transmit information to other battlefields, and me, if necessary." I changed the display and displayed three Frame Gears. Lain's Shining Count was painted pure white. Yae had a Knight Baron that was painted purple, and Elze had a Knight Baron that was painted crimson. They could've had their own comedy routine about three Black Knights that were in no way black at all.

Yae's Frame Gear was equipped with a curved crystal blade, and Elze's was equipped with some crude crystal gauntlets. I'd made both weapons from phrasium. Lain had a similar bladed weapon, as well.

"So, here's how we're going to do this. Assess the situation at your individual locations and act accordingly. If you see anything unusual or suspicious, contact me immediately. In addition, if you see a really fast red Frame Gear, don't worry, he's our ally. Any questions?"

"I've heard there are some airborne Phrase. How should we deal with those?"

"I'll take care of them. Try to avoid taking damage. There are also certain Phrase that might shoot crystal arrows or missiles. If your Frame Gear gets damaged too badly, you'll be sent back here.

But if your cockpit gets destroyed directly, you won't be sent back in time, so keep your guard up." Each commander boarded their respective Black Knights after I explained the strategy. The soldiers split into A Squad, B Squad, and C Squad respectively. Lain then joined A Squad, Yae joined B Squad, and Elze joined C Squad.

Kougyoku, Kohaku, and Kokuyou and Sango boarded with the three respective people as well. They'd be my way of communicating efficiently to each squad. I also had Norn join B Squad, and Nikola join C Squad as backup. Yae and Elze were going to move freely and not focus too heavily on giving orders. That was why I figured it was smarter to have a vice-commander backing each of them up.

I had several Frame Gears, Tsubaki, old man Baba, and a summoned Cerberus stationed at HQ just in case. If anything bad happened, they'd be sure to contact me.

I moved A Squad, B Squad, and C Squad to their respective locations using **[Gate]**.

I joined the battle alongside A Squad. It was time to prepare.

《It's time to begin. I'll be trusting you guys to relay my orders.》

《As you command.》

《Very well, my lord.》

《Sssure thing, darling…》

《Blessings of luck upon you, my master.》 Kohaku, Kougyoku, Kokuyou, and Sango all reported for duty.

I pulled up my map display and confirmed where the Phrase were on the map. Then, I pulled one of the little slides Ende had given me out of my breast pocket.

"…This better actually do something." I knew I'd punch Ende if it was a prank or something. I applied a little force, breaking the slide with a firm snap.

"Huh..." No sound came out. I began suspecting that I'd actually been tricked. I anxiously looked at the map, and found that all the Phrase in Yulong had stopped moving. After a few moments... they all began charging toward me. It had worked, apparently. It seemed that whatever noise the Sovereign made, it was beyond human comprehension.

Of all the Phrase headed our way, some of them were moving faster than others. I had a small idea as to why that was. *Hm... I wonder...*

"Search. Display any flying Phrase with yellow markers."

"Understood. Displaying." The group of Phrase heading our way was quickly dotted with yellow. Luckily, it was as I expected. There weren't many flying enemies at all. There only seemed to be about ten.

Frame Gears couldn't fly, so I had no choice but to take care of them myself. I took out two phrasium greatswords and readied the weapons.

《Kougyoku, I'm going to kill the flying Phrase headed this way. The first ground group should appear in about fifteen minutes.》

《Understood. Please stay safe.》 I sent a telepathic message to Kougyoku, who was with Lain in the White Knight.

"Alright, time to give them a little show." I invoked **[Fly]**, leaped up into the sky, and went barreling off to meet the flying Phrase.

The battle was about to commence.

"Hup!" I passed by some flying Phrase, splitting their cores as I moved on by. One fell, then a second.

A third, and a fourth... I sliced through several of the flying Phrase.

I looked below and saw a group of Phrase kicking up dust as they stampeded. I had no choice but to trust Lain and the others to take care of them. My role, first and foremost, was to kill the flying ones. I was lucky there weren't any flying Intermediate Constructs like the Manta Phrase.

I soared through the sky, took out another group of flying enemies, then zoomed down and killed a bunch on the ground. I focused on wiping out the Lesser Constructs and ignored the larger ones.

I kept my map displayed, constantly tracking their movement. The group furthest away had started heading in this direction. They weren't moving normally... It looked like they were charging full-pelt in our direction.

"The battle at point A will begin soon. I'm heading to point B." Judging from the map situation, almost every Phrase in Yulong was going to converge on Lain's position.

I opened a [Gate] and came out at point B. Yae's group was there, currently on standby. The soldiers from Mismede and Ramissh gave me a hearty welcome.

《I'm about to begin calling the Phrase toward me. Get everyone prepared to fight!》

《As you wish.》 I sent a telepathic message to Kohaku. The plan was to have Kohaku convey the message to Yae, and then have Yae convey the message to the others. I looked over all the Frame Gears brandishing their weapons and felt a faint sense of pride. With that, I took the slide from my breast pocket and snapped it apart.

On my map display, the Phrase moving toward point A split slightly, a group of them now charging in the direction of point

B. About half of them broke off and started heading to my current location. There were no more flying types, so they were all moving at around the same speed.

"Search. Display the current number of Phrase."

"Understood… Search complete. Twelve-thousand-and-seventeen Phrase." The number on the display had already begun decreasing steadily. That was because the battle at point A had already started. If I recalled correctly, there were over thirteen-thousand of them when I'd initially run the search… That meant Ende had killed about a thousand of them on his own.

I used [**Fly**] to perch on the shoulder of Yae's Frame Gear.

"The Phrase should be here in a few minutes, alright? I'll be counting on you."

"I understand, I do. You can count on me." I used [**Gate**] to move toward point C, deciding to check on Elze.

I was greeted by a trio of robots. Elze's crimson Frame Gear, equipped with transparent gauntlets. Monica's scarlet Frame Gear with a huge crystal wrench. Nikola, on the other hand, was piloting a non-custom Black Knight.

《The battle has begun at point A. It's about to start at point B, too. I'll lure the remaining ones here.》

《Understood.》

《Ssssure thing.》 As Sango and Kokuyou replied, I shattered the third slide. A few of the Phrase headed toward point B split off and headed toward point C.

"Hrmph… We didn't attract as many as I expected." My timing for breaking the slide may have been a bit off… The split between the three locations definitely wasn't even.

I looked toward the map and tried to get a feel for the numbers. About fifty percent of all Phrase were headed to point A, thirty percent were en route to point B, and twenty percent were coming toward Point C.

"It's looking like Lain's gonna have the roughest ride..." I decided to send several troops from point C to provide backup at point A. We didn't need as many here, after all.

I stood on the shoulder of Monica's Frame Gear, then barked out commands.

"Monica and twenty Brunhild soldiers will be going to point A! Brace for teleportation, but be aware that the battle has already begun over there."

"Hoh... It's about time they taste the cold sting of my wrench. Uhm, like, Master! Don't even worry about it, I'll kill them all, and stuff!" I opened up a [Gate], sending Monica and twenty soldiers to point A. I came through too, finding them all in the heat of battle.

The soldiers were trashing the Lesser Constructs and cutting them to pieces with weaponry. Then, they turned toward the Intermediate Constructs, focusing their attacks.

"Charge!" I jumped down from the shoulder of Monica's Frame Gear, lunging at an incoming Phrase. The soldiers around me all ran forward into battle, slaying several Lesser Constructs in a flash.

"Outta the way, and stuff!" Monica swung down her wrench against the torso of an Intermediate Construct. It smashed into pieces, and she stomped its core in an instant. Then, her leg continued its momentum, smashing into several smaller ones.

I didn't want to get hit, so I moved away from the middle of the fray and picked off a few smaller ones myself. I looked at the counter on the map and it was already down to ten-thousand-eight-hundred-and-fifty-two.

The battle at point B had begun, too. The battle at point C wasn't far off, either. I needed to wipe out the little ones as swiftly as possible. Suddenly, a telepathic message came in from Kougyoku.

《My liege. Regulus Unit Fifteen has taken severe damage. It has to withdraw.》

What?! I pulled up the map and headed toward the area. I found a Chevalier with a shattered leg and a sliced-apart arm rolling around on the ground. Its head was completely smashed as well.

I got closer and opened up the chest hatch, just to ensure the guy wasn't still stuck in there. Fortunately, it was empty. It seemed as though he had been properly sent back to HQ.

I used [**Storage**] to contain the broken Frame Gear. As I did that, I received another message.

《Master, sir! Regulus Fifteen says he can return to the front!》

《What's his condition?》

《He's all good! He got up and said he wants to fight again, sir!》

《Got it. Have him on standby to ship out again, then.》 The Cerberus I had stationed at HQ relayed Rosetta's voice. I was relieved to hear the pilot was alright.

I used [**Gate**] to summon him and his new Frame Gear back to the battlefield within seconds.

The Chevalier he was riding was identical to the previous one in every way... Except for one. The purple number on his shoulder had been hastily scrawled on at the last minute.

Still, current circumstances didn't call for differentiating people too much, so how he looked wasn't a big deal.

Regulus Unit Fifteen bowed to me briefly and went right back to smashing monsters.

It didn't take long for all the Intermediate Constructs to fall, and then it was a case of mopping up the Lesser Constructs. If a

Frame Gear was the size of a person, then the Lesser Constructs here were about the size of an average dog. Several of them shattered to pieces every time a soldier swung down his weapon.

《The next wave is set to arrive in about five minutes. Everyone can take a brief rest, but get ready to fight again at a moment's notice.》

《Got it!》 I sent a telepathic message to Kougyoku, who was accompanying Lain. Then, I opened up a **[Gate]** to point C and made my way there.

In a stark contrast to the other two locations, there weren't many enemies at point C at all. I considered sending some troops elsewhere.

But still, the battle at point C had begun as well. Several Frame Gears cornered the Intermediate Constructs and began ganging up on them. The Lesser Constructs had no chances here, either.

I dived into the fray and took out a bunch of smaller ones as well. Still, for every one I killed, two more took their place.

《My liege... Ramissh Unit Eleven is badly damaged.》 Kohaku's voice echoed in my head. That was all the way at Point B. I was really being pushed hard... I'd only just arrived at point C and I already had to backtrack.

I flew back to Point B, collected the broken Frame Gear, and redeployed Ramissh Unit Eleven.

I glanced at the Phrase counter, finding it had decreased to nine-thousand-and-forty-three. That was great news, since it meant we'd already killed over a thousand of them.

The situation was tough, but it looked like we would surely prevail.

I killed, killed, and killed some more. I smashed as many Phrase as I could as I soared through the air.

When I wasn't killing, I was picking up trashed Frame Gears and sending out the reserve units.

Thankfully, there were no casualties, but a lot of people had gotten concussions due to the impact of falling in their Frame Gears. Sure they could be treated back at HQ, but our numbers were slowly but surely dropping.

It was no surprise that our forces grew fatigued as we were faced with overwhelming odds. Every man had to kill fifty Phrase, so the deck was stacked against us.

The map confirmed that even more waves of enemies were inbound to all three points, as well. The number of Phrase had already been reduced to around five-thousand, but our soldiers were rapidly reaching their limits.

"Haaah!" Elze's fist shattered the body of an Intermediate Construct, catching its core and smashing it with a leg sweep. Refreese's vice-commander, specially equipped with a phrasium spear, pierced another one and skewered its core.

I hopped on top of the vice-commander's Frame Gear and called out to him.

"Ah, pardon me. There aren't many left here, so I'll be sending you and the other Refreese units to point B."

"Very well. Give us a moment." The voice blaring through the speakers suddenly paused, then the surrounding Refreese knights piloted their Frame Gears in my direction.

I moved seventeen of them in total toward point B. I stayed on the vice-commander's shoulder, so I went through with them.

Point B was in the midst of a heated battle, and the combined forces of Ramissh and Mismede were giving the Phrase a good run for their money. Refreese's soldiers wasted no time in joining in.

A nearby Chevalier struck a Phrase with his mace, deftly blocking a crystal arrow with its shield at the same time. The blow made several cracks along the creature's surface, and the other heavy knights followed up with swings of their own. It seemed almost cruel to look at, like they were bullying the poor thing... But it was a simple matter of kill or be killed.

A bunch of Lesser Constructs moved in to jump up at the soldiers. The Heavy Knights repelled them with ease, shattering them with their large weapons.

They clearly knew how to handle themselves, but the soldiers were showing signs of fatigue. Their movements were getting subtly slower by the minute.

"Huh?" A red Frame Gear suddenly burst onto the scene at intense speed. It wasn't Elze. Elze was at point C, and I was currently at point B. I figured it was Ende.

I thought he'd hide and run away the moment the actual battle began... Seems I'd underestimated the value of his word.

He danced wildly, flourishing the twin blades and slaughtering every Phrase in his path. He aimed with frightening precision, striking the cores of each deliberately and swiftly. The guy far outclassed every other fighter on the field.

As I flew over to Ende's Frame Gear, the hatch opened up and he revealed himself to me.

"Yo, Touya. I'm thinking about heading off soon, is that okay?"

"Honestly, you've already helped me more than I expected, so that should be fine."

"No, no... See, there's something I have to attend to. I can't keep helping since I'll run outta time. Anyway, I came by to warn you." Ende raised a single finger, smiling devilishly at me as he spoke.

Huh? A warning?

"Yeah... An Upper Construct is coming. Y'know, one of the real big boys. It's not in this world yet, but it's going to breach in the north-west. I'd expect it to hit in about five minutes. You should probably issue a retreat if you care about your people and their safety."

"What...?!" *An Upper Construct?! Wasn't that like one of the strongest of the Phrase?!*

"Why's there one of those here?!"

"You know, I'm not actually too sure. It's probably because so many poured out at once. The tear they made is big enough to allow an Upper through, and... here we are! Don't worry though, the seam will start getting smaller the moment it passes into this world, so don't expect another to come through any time soon."

His words were hardly comforting. I didn't know why he was acting so nonchalant.

"Well, best of luck! Later, Touya."

"H-Hey now!" In a matter of seconds, both Ende and his Dragoon vanished into nothingness. He'd used his teleportation magic... But it wasn't the time to think about that.

《Kohaku! Evacuate everyone in the north-western area! There's an Upper Construct coming! Hurry!》

《Wha—?! I-I understand!》 Kohaku conveyed the information, and all the Frame Gears in the northwest started pulling back one by one. They didn't waste any opportunity, however, and smashed several Lesser Constructs on their way back. The number on the map had dropped down to two-thousand-five-hundred-and-seventeen. I was honestly impressed. We'd been fighting for around three hours, and everyone was getting pretty damn tired. I had no idea if they'd be able to handle an enemy like this. Without warning, a vibration ran through the air. The atmosphere itself felt as though it were quaking. As the air began to shudder, vibrant cracks appeared in the very space before my eyes.

The crack ran and spread across reality itself, a two-dimensional pattern somehow imprinting on three-dimensional space. A snapping sound rang out through the area, and an enormous claw appeared out of nothingness.

Almost as though bursting from the fabric of the sky itself, the beast began to break through. Within the warped reality visible through the crack, I saw it.

If I had to define it at a glance, I'd call it a crocodile. Well, it was a six-legged crocodile with a giant horn on its head. It also had things jutting out of the tip of its tail, and a dorsal fin on its back.

It had the same crystalline body as all the other Phrase I'd encountered, but its body structure was clearly far more complicated. There were three glowing cores inside its body, its jagged armor cut clean in straight lines.

If I were to describe it in one word, I would have used monstrous. It was absolutely goddamn gigantic. The Intermediate Phrase were small compared to it, and it made even Frame Gears look tiny.

I suppose if I were to make it a metaphor... If the Crocodile Phrase were the size of a regular Phrase, then the Frame Gears would be the size of a small plastic robot. It was the biggest thing I'd ever seen.

"Th-This is... way too big... C-C'mon now..." I silently swallowed, staring with wide eyes. I didn't think even for a moment that we could defeat it.

While we stared at it like gawping idiots, the crystal croc opened its mouth. Light itself began to collect within its mouth, shimmering and shining in a massive ball. *Shit! It's like that time with the Manta Phrase!*

《Kohaku! Evacuate everyone in front of its mouth, now!》

《Huh?》

Shit, there's no time!

"Gah!" I invoked **[Gate]**, forcefully and without warning shifting every soldier in front of that thing next to me.

I did it just in time, as moments later a beam of raw energy shot in a straight line from its mouth.

SHAKOOOOOOOOOOM! The ray shot forward, burning away everything in its path. Even the ground itself was eroded away in an instant. Everything in its path was atomized, burned away without a trace.

What the hell kind of weapon is that…? It's just like the Charged Particle Cannon from that anime… Though it's not powered by electricity…

It was similar to the Manta Phrase in that it needed time to charge up, but the difference in firepower was nothing to laugh at. If someone was hit by that, there wouldn't be anything left to recover.

…This was the fearsome power of an Upper Construct.

I took out a radio transmitter from **[Storage]** and tuned it to the common channel. I didn't want to cause any political concerns. I was the head of a nation, so issuing commands to foreign soldiers could be interpreted strangely. For that reason, my radio relayed orders only to the commanders of each nation, and they passed it on to their respective armies. All the Frame Gears were within comms range.

"Attention all Brunhild pilots! Don't stand in front of the Upper Construct Phrase! There's a cue to look out for before it launches its attack, but it could still easily crush you by moving around, so keep your distance!" With a rumbling, the Frame Gears moved from the front of the Phrase to its back.

Almost as if waiting for that motion, the Crocodile Phrase rolled to the side, cracking its tail like a whip and striking one of the Chevaliers.

With a tremendous crunching sound, the Heavy Knight was obliterated. It rolled and tumbled on the ground, crumbling to pieces on impact.

《HQ, come in! We have a man down, did the teleport work?!》

《Touya, it's Yumina. The pilot was successfully sent here, but he's gravely injured. Flora's treating him, but he looks like a twisted mess...》 Yumina transmitted a psychic message to me through Cerberus, who was guarding her. Thankfully, the man hadn't died instantly.

The stupid crocodile wriggled its tail left and right, staring us down as if attempting to threaten us. He wasn't particularly fast, though.

If it kept up that pace, it wouldn't be hard to avoid.

However, just as I sank into that kind of relaxed train of thought, several spiked protrusions appeared at the tip of its tail, and then they began launching rapidly like missiles.

"[Shield]!" An invisible shield covered my surroundings, repelling the crystal rain of arrows. All the other Frame Gears held fast with their shields as well, enduring it somehow.

"Wh-What the hell... It's got a cluster bomb attack?!" A cluster bomb was designed for focused assaults. Inside the main blast were several smaller blasts.

It wasn't an attack that marked targets like aiming with a bow, or the kind where you drew a line on your target like firing a machine gun. It was one that covered a wide area. And there was nothing more troubling in their situation.

The spines that it had fired out had already begun regenerating.

That tail's a real pain in the ass... I should probably focus on taking it out... Wait, no. It's still a Phrase, so it'd just grow back.

As I spent my time thinking, the Crocodile Phrase started stomping forward.

"**[Slip]!**" I removed the friction on the ground below all six of its legs. In a flash, the Crocodile Phrase tumbled over with a massive crash. But, as it fell its tail started thrashing around and firing out more missiles.

"Gah, shit!" As we endured the crystal rain once more, it looked right at us. Phrase didn't have eyes, but I swear we were in its sight. It managed to right itself, and opened up its mouth slowly. Light began to gather inside its gaping maw. *Hell no!*

"All units, fan out! Get out of there!" I didn't even need to say anything. The Heavy Knights were already desperately charging away.

Just as before, it roared, a condensed beam of light shooting out before our eyes. It dug the ground out for miles in a straight line. I looked in the distance, and I saw a mountain disappear. *Just how much power does it have...?! Nobody's hurt, but... what do I do?!*

How can I beat it...? It's a Phrase, so I just need to destroy those three cores, but how am I supposed to do that?

Its body is way too big... There's too much thick material in the way... I could probably cut it if I made a fifty-meter sword or something...

There were a lot of materials around, that was true. However, what I lacked was time. Making a blade like that with [**Modeling**] would definitely take me at least an hour. Plus, I didn't even know how to swing something so huge. I considered launching it into the sky with a [**Gate**] like I did with the Mithril Golem, but even if that harmed it, it'd just regenerate again.

The Crocodile Phrase swept to the side and lashed with its tail once more, swatting at us as if we were ants. Multiple Heavy Knights got caught up in the attack.

And, like clockwork, a rain of crystal came pouring down at us. Its attack was pretty plain, but effective. Everyone managed to hold out with their shields, but their pauldrons and legs still took minor damage. Over time, it would definitely chip away at them. There was no avoiding that.

"We can't keep taking attacks like this…! Everyone, group up and strike as one!" I held crystal blades in both of my hands, soaring through the air to the crocodile's flank. Through its body I could make out a core, about one meter in diameter. It faintly shone.

"Take thiiis!!" I struck it in a cross motion, swiping repeatedly with the swords in my hands. Still, no matter what I did, I couldn't reach the core. If this Phrase was a crocodile, then I was a mere fly attempting to pierce its hide.

Suddenly, a screeching pulse echoed out from its dorsal fin, and in a few moments I was blown away.

"Wha…!" I spun around in the sky and recovered my stance. There wasn't any damage. I wasn't hit, but it took me by surprise. Apparently it was capable of generating shockwaves, too. Right on cue, the crystal arrows rained down from the heavens again. Everyone's shields looked close to breaking. The only solace in this attack was that it struck both friend and foe alike.

Ever since it started using that attack, most of the weaker Phrase in the area had taken considerable damage.

If I had to classify this one, it was clear it specialized in extermination. The situation wasn't looking good for us. I had to think of something...

This crystal rain's the worst... It's like a goddamn meteor storm... Oh, wait a second...!

I looked around the area. There were shards of shattered Phrase scattered all over the place. I wondered if I could do it.

"Soldiers, do you copy? I need you to buy me three minutes of time. There's no need to engage the enemy. Just draw its attention and keep it occupied." It looked like they got my message. All the knights began to move in unison, attempting to divert its attention away from me.

Alright, better take my shot... I used [**Multiple**] and [**Transfer**] to pour vast quantities of magic into the scattered Phrase pieces in the area. I made them considerably tougher than the Upper Construct's shell.

"All units, fan out! Get as far away from the big one as possible!" Everyone moved away after receiving my message. Once I confirmed their safety, I opened up a [**Gate**] and moved all the scattered fragments into the sky far above the Crocodile Phrase. The pieces were dozens of meters up in the air. I didn't want to make it too high, or the aim would be off.

"Take this, you bastard! [**Meteor Rain**]!"

I applied [**Gravity**] to the Phrase fragments in the sky. I multiplied their weight by a magnitude of tens of thousands.

The glimmering fragments of pure destruction rained down upon the massive beast, pelting devastating blasts into its massive body.

Several fragments embedded themselves in the crocodile's body, creating cracks along the surface of its back. I kept on channeling **[Gravity]**, making them heavier and heavier.

The monstrously large crocodile was pinned to the ground, exuding a noise similar to that of nails on a chalkboard.

The sound of splintering and cracking rang out as more of its body fragmented. Apparently the magic I had poured in wasn't quite enough. I increased the weight even further.

The cracks found each other, creating even larger cracks.

The Crocodile Phrase attempted to open its maw and fire out its light blast, but its mouth was damaged by the fragments as well, so it couldn't open up properly. I heard loud sounds of creaking and straining from the body of the beast.

"Break to pieces, you bastard!" I increased the weight once more, just to be sure. The fragments sank in even deeper. Finally, unable to bear any more strain, the crocodile smashed into thousands of pieces like a glass ornament falling from a great height.

"Now, swarm it! Destroy the cores before it can regenerate! There should be three!" All the soldiers charged toward the newly-exposed cores, striking them with their weapons. One of them shattered almost immediately, vanishing in seconds. The other two quickly followed suit, crumbling to nothingness under the relentless assault. With that, the Upper Construct had been reduced to a mountain of raw materials.

"Hoooraaah!!!" All the soldiers from Mismede, Ramissh, Refreese, and Brunhild let our cheers, waving their weapons overhead all the while.

There were still a few Phrase remaining, but point B was pretty much cleared out.

Somehow, we'd managed. I used more magic than I expected. In fact, it was probably the most magic I'd ever used in a single fight. Still, I knew it was ultimately necessary in order to take care of the Upper Construct.

"The Brunhild knight order can take care of the rest from here. Mismede, Ramissh, prepare for warp to point A. Brace for transfer… Now's the time we end this!"

"Hurrah!" Almost every Frame Gear present at point B warped off to point A. It seemed like the troops at point C had everything under control as well. I looked at the remaining Phrase in Yulong. There were only four-hundred-and-seventy-eight left. It was no longer a war, but more a matter of cleanup.

We'd scaled a mountain in terms of effort. But we'd actually done it. We'd successfully repelled an invasion. Still, I couldn't get cocky just yet. After all, I definitely couldn't say I saved Yulong.

The Upper Construct launched out that beam after I slipped it, so people could've been caught up in that.

"…Thinking about it won't change anything." I opened up [Storage] and picked up all the fragments. My spoils of war, the greatest haul yet.

"Yae, Norn, I'll leave the rest here to you. I'm headed to point A."

"Very well, Touya-dono."

"Roger dodger!" I took a detour before heading to point A, dropping in back at HQ. Linze saw me arrive, rushing over to me immediately.

"Touya, are you alright?!"

"…Yeah, I think so. I'm just exhausted." I was pushed to the brink, both physically and mentally. I'd definitely gone a little far with my magical usage.

Lu brought me a chair, and I sank right into it.

Ah... I need to clear my head... I can't think straight right now.

《Touya, do you hear me?》

《Elze? Something wrong?》 I raised my head. *Please don't tell me we've got two more Upper Constructs or something...*

《We cleared out as many Phrase as we could find, but I just want you to check if there are any left...》

《Hm? Ah... Gimme a minute.》 I pulled up the map, finding no Phrase presence at point C anymore. There were only Phrase remaining at locations A and B. There were two-hundred-and-forty-seven left in total.

《It's all good. No more Phrase where you are. Come back to HQ with the rest of your squad.》

《Got it!》 All the soldiers at point C were brought back to HQ. As I did that, the Phrase at point B were wiped out, leaving only the ones at point A.

Slowly, their numbers dwindled too, and it eventually reached zero. Everyone looking at the display cheered.

At my HQ, borders had no meaning. Soldiers from various countries hugged one another and celebrated with each other. They all cheered as one.

《Attention everyone! Mission success. All Phrase have been annihilated. I'm calling you all back to HQ. Good work!》 The Frame Gears all appeared at HQ one by one, opening up so their pilots could clamber out and celebrate.

Some of them got overexcited and ended up leaping out of the cockpits, hurting themselves in the process.

"Good work... Everyone... Gh..." I felt like a dead man walking. I was about ready to sleep like a log, but I still had a few things to take care of.

First thing to do was to collect all the shattered Phrase fragments, then I had to return everyone to their respective countries, and then I had to put all the Frame Gears back in the hangar... That was all my responsibility.

What do I do after that again...? Oh, right... I better check on Yulong's heavenly emperor... I pulled up my map, but for some reason Shenghai wasn't listed. *Huh... What's the deal here...? Is my app bugged?*

A sudden thought entered my mind, so I moved to look at point B on the map. Then, I calculated the trajectory of the beam the Crocodile Phrase had fired. My discovery was grim. The line of fire overlapped with the former location of Shenghai on my map.

In other words, as a result of that blast... Shenghai, Yulong's capital, had been wiped clean from the face of the world.

A few days passed after that. We ended up with thirty-six severely damaged Frame Gears, twenty-four people with minor injuries, four people with life-threatening injuries, and no casualties at all.

It was great that we hadn't lost anyone in the fight, but the picture on a whole was rather grim.

Yulong's capital was completely wiped out, and various towns and villages were erased from the map entirely. I couldn't help but feel we could've had a better result if we were a little more skilled in our approach.

"So, what happens to Yulong now?"

"That's hard to say. I'd prefer not to get involved any further, though. Ain't really my business to begin with." Of all the western alliance leaders, the beastking spoke up half-heartedly.

"Will other countries start contesting Yulong's territory now? It'd be bad if wars started happening. The people of Yulong have suffered enough…"

"Well, with regards to Hannock, they've had no interest in Yulong from the start, so they should be fine. Xenoahs has a strict policy about not interfering with human affairs, so that's also alright. There's a lot of civil unrest in Eashen, so they aren't unified enough to start a land grab… And apparently the Kingdom of Horn opposes militaristic invasion as a matter of national principle."

"So that just leaves Felsen, Nokia, and Roadmare…" The king of Belfast and the emperor of Regulus both chimed in after the pope's concern.

"In my opinion, those three nations will likely play a waiting game and see how things go for a while. Think about it like this… Mysterious invaders simply came from nowhere and delivered sheer devastation to Yulong. Would you want to govern a place like that without waiting to see if it was safe first? Even thinking about that happening within my own territory makes my blood run cold…" The emperor of Refreese raised a fair point as well. It would only be natural to expect something like this to happen again.

"So… does Yulong currently lack a leader?"

"No, quite the contrary. The heavenly emperor had three sons. One of those lived in Shenghai and shared his fate. Another was in another city, but it was ravaged by the Phrase and he succumbed. The third son survived and is calling himself the new rightful heavenly emperor." The king of Belfast turned to the king of Lihnea, answering his question. It hadn't taken long for a new heavenly emperor to show up. I hoped that he'd be able to set Yulong on the right path.

But, as I had such hopeful thoughts, the king of Belfast made an irritated face.

"Unfortunately... according to reports, the new heavenly emperor is claiming that Yulong was destroyed as an act of war by the Duchy of Brunhild... He claims you are directly responsible, Touya."

"Wait, what?!" *How the hell could he say that?!* I silently stared, mouth agape. I couldn't comprehend why someone would make up a story like that.

"The story goes that the Phrase are mighty beasts created by a unique summoning spell you employed after attacking Shenghai. He's using the great wall you built on the Hannock border as evidence of your magical potential. Furthermore, there are people whispering that you fueled your magic with blood... More specifically, the blood of the innocent Yulong citizens. They claim that you sacrificed and harvested the population to create more monsters, and there are even people claiming to have seen you doing this."

What the hell?! Come on, that's total bull! That just sounds like trashy gossip! Who the hell said they saw me summoning those things, huh?!

"You seem pretty acquainted with the rumors already, how come?"

"Well, they actually contacted us formally. We received a letter stating that the entire thing was orchestrated by you, and that they are innocent victims of your savage power play. They also claim that you are attempting to showcase your military might across the world, so that none may oppose you."

"Indeed, we also received a letter. It said something to the effect of Brunhild cannot be allowed to possess such strength. Therefore, it should be confiscated and safely claimed by larger nations like Belfast, Regulus, and Yulong." After the king of Belfast spoke up, the emperor of Regulus chimed in as well. I was amazed that the new heavenly emperor was actually trying this kind of underhanded approach.

"So, what are you gonna tell them?"

"Nothing, really. If I were to reply, I'd tell them that it wouldn't be possible for us to rival Brunhild, and that we wouldn't be prepared to face an enemy that could wipe Yulong's capital off the map. I don't really know what they were expecting, but under ordinary circumstances, I would have suggested surrendering."

"In my case, I probably shouldn't leave it alone. I'll tell them that I'll show the letter to the grand duke to confirm the truth, but warn them that the grand duke of Brunhild has a terribly short temper and may storm Yulong if there's a mistake. I'll just reiterate that it's my national duty to seek out the truth, and to leave everything to me."

These two... Kinda feels like they're shirking the responsibility here... Well, whatever. I guess I can sympathize, since they didn't really ask for this nonsense.

Still, I'm a little worried... I don't think a standard Yulong citizen would be able to tell it was a lie...

Now, come on... I guess they might not all be like that. The upper class of Yulong is definitely rotten, but I'm sure their people won't fall for such nonsense. I hope...

"In the meantime, we should probably leave Yulong be. In its current state, they won't be able to take much action, and it's not like any of us share a border with them." The king of Lihnea raised a fair point as well. Yulong no longer had the same national or military power as before.

I didn't think Hannock had any intention of fighting them, either, so I decided to hand the border wall over to them. Leaving Yulong alone was the smartest course of action. That was what I decided. We were to no longer interfere with that country and generally ignore any nonsense the new heavenly king came out with.

That guy had pretty much destroyed all credibility with the western alliance thanks to his lies. I wish he'd had some honest people serving him, but I guess the new government was just as corrupt. I suppose the old saying was true, like father like son.

Two weeks later, the heavenly emperor of Yulong was assassinated. Amongst the remaining nobility of the nation, there was an intense power play ending in several deaths. Many nobles ended up announcing that they were the real heavenly emperor, and ended up killing one another in paranoia.

Various citizens from Yulong became refugees after the crisis, fleeing the ravaged nation and taking up nomadic lives.

Ultimately, the assassination of the heavenly emperor was blamed on me. I'd really had enough of that stupid country.

"So, what happened then?"

"Nothing. People can say what they want. If you entertain their stupidity, you've already lost."

"Hmph… But Touyaaa… Taking on a stupid country like Yulong would totally be a piece of cake for a guy like you!" Sue was sitting on my lap, treating me much like a chair. She was acting a little fussy.

I was hanging out with her since she hadn't visited in a while, but once I started talking about Yulong she got a little mad.

"Plus, didn't you actually save Yulong?! Why are they blaming you? They're just making up whatever's best for them! But even worse than that, they aren't acting on these rumors! They're just barking without biting!"

"Well, it's best to just leave it be... It'll only get more annoying."

"No way! That's not enough! You gotta get mad at times like these, Touya! If you don't get serious and show them what you're made of, they'll just keep mocking you! If you sit there like a doormat, don't be surprised when they walk all over you! If you don't smack them in the face, they're just gonna think they can keep doing it...!"

Man, you're getting pretty mad about it... Guess she learned a lot about diplomacy from her dad.

"So, what course of action would you suggest?"

"Strike down all those 'new' heavenly emperors with all you've got! Publicly humiliate them and tell them to stop those rumors for good!"

...Definitely not taking that diplomatic approach. It's a little... childish, to handle things in a manner like that.

Still, it was a little cute that she got mad on my behalf. I gently patted Sue on the head, smiling softly at her fussy face.

"Thanks, really... But it's alright, Sue. I promise."

"…You're way too kind, Touya. It's one of the loveliest things about you… but don't let people take advantage of you, okay?" Sue turned around and hugged me tight, rubbing her face against my chest. I smiled, pulling her gently against me and rubbing her back. I felt warm and safe with her.

I suddenly heard the door creak, and I looked upward. Cesca peeked into the room, strolling in with some tea.

"…I've brought tea for you, my cradle-robbing master."

"…I need to talk to you right now, maid."

No, this isn't what it looks like. I swear! Me hugging Sue isn't anything sexual, it's entirely wholesome and familial! It's not perverse at all… For the time being, at least… No, wait!

"There's no need to sneak around in private so late, you know? Little old Cesca knows well the naughty disposition of her lecherous master… Please, act as though I'm not here. Indulge your savage urges to your heart's content."

"Come here, damn it! I need to talk to you about your conduct."

"Oh, you're going to teach me a lesson, Master…?"

"Enough, get over here!"

I lectured that stupid pervy maid for about an hour after that… But during the lecture, all she did was blush and say stuff like "Berate me harder." In the end, I got annoyed with her and gave up. I didn't have any time for her nonsense.

I left the castle, abandoning Cesca to her delusions. Earlier that day, I'd formally given Sue a ring, marking our engagement, but that wasn't all I wanted to do with her. I decided that it was time to show her Babylon. I didn't want her to be out of the loop, and I had no reason not to trust her. Though, I did reiterate how she couldn't tell anyone at all under any circumstances. Better safe than sorry.

I fired up a **[Gate]** and took Sue through. She opened her eyes in wonder as she looked up into the sky from Babylon's grounds.

"Ohmygosh! Wow! Wowowow! It's so cool! The castle in the sky was real the whole time!"

Well, it's a little different from that place... For one, it isn't in ruins. Sue got even more excited once we reached the rampart's castle.

"An indeedious welcome to you, master."

"Oh, hey Liora. Where's Noel?"

"She is indeed in the midst of an after-snack nap."

Again...? Man, that girl sure likes napping, I think she only actually wakes up during mealtime.

"Who's that, Touya?"

"This is Preliora. She's the one in charge of the rampart. She doesn't come down too often, so I'm not surprised you haven't met her."

"Indeed, I am Preliora. But you may call me Liora, thank you." Liora gently curtseyed in Sue's direction with a faint smile. Of all the Babylon Gynoids, she certainly exuded the most dignified air. She was definitely more like an elder sister.

"Liora. Any word on the new system?"

"Indeed. I have indeed spoken with Rosetta about it, and implementation seems to be possible. I must confess I never once considered implementing satellite orb technology into the Frame Gears." The satellite orb was one of Babylon's primary defensive systems. It was composed of several orichalcum spheres that moved autonomously and intercepted enemies.

I got the idea of tweaking it a bit and making a localized version for Frame Gears. In other words, it was an attack drone system that individual Frame Gears could deploy at will. I was inspired by some of my favorite anime, of course.

Rather than orbs, these orbital drones would be in the shape of swords, and they'd be constructed out of Phrase fragments. As an aside, calling them Phrase fragments all the time was kind of a pain, so that was why I'd taken to calling the material phrasium. They were small enough for the workshop to mass-produce efficiently, as well.

Their combat efficiency would be directly tied to the pilot's aptitude for magic. How long they could operate for would also be tied to the user's magic power. Not everyone would be able to make proper use, but the addition of a ranged attack in any form was certainly a welcome one.

I decided to name my new drone system Fragarach. It was simply the first name that came to mind. I didn't really need to worry about people questioning it. The origin of that name wasn't from this world, after all.

Going by the control systems of all the current Frame Gears, they could handle up to four each at a time.

Unfortunately, the blueprints for the upgraded Frame Gears were in the storehouse, which I still hadn't found. What a bother…

A month had passed since the Phrase invasion, and nothing odd had happened since then.

The guildmaster, Relisha, did show up and ask for an explanation of what exactly went down. Apparently there was a branch in Yulong that got completely trashed.

The civil war, if you could even call it that, was continuing in Yulong. Every now and then a new noble would appear and claim he was the rightful heavenly emperor, only to be killed by another noble declaring *himself* as the true heavenly emperor, and so on.

Yulong itself was no longer a unified country; it had broken down into several city states within the former country's territory. It would be more apt to call it the "Yulong Region," as it no longer had any singular national identity. I wondered if they'd do what the nearby Roadmare Union did, and eventually form a unified alliance amongst the smaller states.

"Those arrogant idiots won't last long if they pursue spring dreams."

"Hm? What do you mean?"

"I'm saying that no matter how they prosper, they obviously wouldn't have lasted forever. Just like a little dream in the midst of early spring, their ideals are fleeting." Monica looked confused at my explanation, so I just went about and dropped it. After thinking about it, I realized Yulong had probably lasted a long time as a nation, so my musing wasn't exactly on point.

The fact that Yulong was destroyed by mysterious invaders didn't take long to spread to other nations.

In the end, not quite as many Yulong nobles continued to slander me as I'd expected. Plus, I had the guild help mitigate the damage by distributing flyers and information to adventurers. The information concerned the Phrase, explaining what they looked like, what they were called, and the fact that they had ravaged the world in the past.

I also disclosed their strengths and weaknesses. I was hoping that adventuring parties would be able to take out Lesser Constructs if they were equipped with that information.

We had no idea where they'd appear next, after all. It was necessary to finally make them public knowledge.

Still, if I was to believe what Ende had told me, I wouldn't have to worry about another grand invasion for a while.

"So then, we can only have four Fragarach drones equipped to a Frame Gear at once?"

"Sir yes sir! If we equip any more, then the Frame Gear's mobility will be hindered, sir!" That certainly wasn't something we wanted. A Frame Gear that couldn't move well might as well have been a sitting duck. The four-drone limit had nothing to do with the pilot, it was simply a technical limitation of the outdated Frame Gear schematics we had on hand.

Rosetta had just finished installing four Fragarachs onto a Knight Baron, so she promptly descended from its shoulder.

They were arranged in a cross-shape on its back. Since they were sword-shaped and made out of phrasium, they could also be used as conventional weapons in a pinch.

Using a Fragarach to attack was something that consumed exhaustive amounts of energy, so it wasn't something I could have people use consecutively. I'd asked if we could use **[Transfer]** in advance to give the pilots more to work with, but apparently after synchronizing with the pilot's wavelength, the Frame Gear would either reject my magic, or make it so only I could control the Fragarach drones. Neither were particularly appealing.

We'd finished making the new weapon, but there was certainly a lot to consider about it...

《My liege, is everything well...?》

《Hm? Kohaku? I'm alright. Something going on with you?》 Kohaku was currently back at the royal castle, so I was surprised to receive a telepathic message.

《Representatives from a foreign nation have arrived at the castle. They're seeking an audience with you.》

《Foreign representatives? If they're from Yulong, just chase them the hell out already.》

《They're certainly not from Yulong. They appear to be from, er... a place called Lestia. Some kind of Knight Kingdom.》

Oh, that sounds familiar... Wasn't that the place where I flew over and helped that Hildegard girl fight against some Phrase...? Yeah, now I remember! I saved her and gave her a phrasium sword. She did say something or other about making it up to me, I think... I wonder if this is it! I used **[Gate]** to go to my throne room, but nobody was there. *What the heck?*

"Ah, Your Majesty. Please, this way." I was looking around the room like a moron when Lapis showed up and beckoned me to follow.

"Didn't we have a group from Lestia here?"

"Yes, we did... But when I asked them to wait a while, they headed for the training grounds to watch our knight order practice their swordplay." *Huh, that makes sense. If they're from the Knight Kingdom, they've gotta love a good fight. I can understand why they might wanna watch foreign soldiers display their skills, too. So long as they're just watching, it's no biggie.*

I arrived at the training grounds to find Logan and a female knight dueling with training swords. But that wasn't just any female knight. It was Princess Hildegard! I had no idea how to react.

"Haaah!!!" The knight princess delivered the final blow, screaming loudly as she disarmed her foe. Logan's sword flew up into the air. She was pretty damn talented, that was for sure.

"Match concluded!" Nikola's voice reverberated through the field. The crowd, huddled around and watching the fight intently, erupted into cheering. I could see members of my knight order, as well as Lestian knights.

"Th-Thank you so much, venerable princess..."

"And to you." The two exchanged pleasantries, and with that the match was over. Just as I'd wondered if she'd spotted me, I saw the girl pick up the pace and head in my direction. Her long blonde hair shimmered as it blew in the gentle wind. She was clad in her usual armor, but had the sweetest little smile on her face. Now that I had a better look at her, she looked to be around Yae's age.

"Y-Your Highness... I-It's been a while!"

"Yep, sure has. But uh, more to the point... what're you doing here, Princess Hildegard?" I returned her greeting, but was mostly just surprised to see her.

"This visit is my way of saying thanks for that incident. There's also something I wished to ask of you... Still, I'm not here as the representative, but more of an attendant."

"...Attendant to who, exactly?"

"That would be me." An elderly fellow stepped out from the gathering of Lestian knights. He looked close to seventy years old. He had a long white mustache on his face, and hobbled along with a gnarled cane. Even though he walked with a cane, his back was completely straight. He had an excellent poise about him and seemed fit for his age. Suddenly, I had a thought as to who he might be...

"It is a pleasure to make your acquaintance, Grand Duke of Brunhild. My name is Galen Yunas Lestia. I am the former king of Lestia, and a Gold-ranked adventurer, much like you." The old man took a guild card from his pocket, presenting it to me. It was definitely the real deal. I was pretty sure this guy was the only other person on the planet to share my rank.

"It's a pleasure, sir. I'm Mochizuki Touya. I've heard about you before. Guildmaster Relisha spoke well of you."

"Ohohohohohhh... You have my gratitude, young man. You brought us something wonderful recently. I was wondering if I might be able to confer my thanks, and make my way around Brunhild to see what this fine nation has to show for itself."

"I guess that could be arranged...? There's not a lot going on in terms of sightseeing, but you'd be an honored guest if you decided to stay here a while." I reached out to shake the former king's hand, but somehow... I missed. *Wait, what?*

"Eeek!!" I turned around in response to the sudden scream, only to find Lapis clutching her behind and shuddering violently. The former king had somehow flash-stepped behind her, and was making a groping motion with his palm.

What.

"Oh, you must forgive me… This is just a habitual manner of mine. Goodness me… What an exceptionally firm ass. I can tell you're no mere maid, since it's toned to perfection."

"G-Grandfather, please! We're guests, this is not Lestia! H-Have some restraint…!"

"You'll have to forgive me, my hand moves on instinct when it senses a righteous rump. I've been rather patient until now, restraining myself in a magnificent sea of asses, but I'm almost at my limit, you know? Bwahahahaah…" Hildegard suddenly got mad at the former king. That was a little jarring. Given her response, I had to assume his behavior here wasn't out of the norm. If I recalled correctly, she seemed a little reserved when I'd mentioned the former king during our last meeting. Now I understood why.

But more importantly, I had no idea how or when he'd gotten past me. Lapis was also a former member of Espion, and was a fully trained spy, so it made no sense that he'd gotten behind her with such precision and speed.

The old man was absolutely not an ordinary person. He clearly had his Gold rank for a reason. Then again, he could've just been exceptionally talented at being a pervert.

"Please forgive us! This is just… my grandfather's reflexes taking hold. O-Once he's touched you, he'll generally leave you alone, so don't worry."

"Hah… Goodness me…" *What the hell kind of reflex is that supposed to be? I can't believe this guy ruled over a kingdom of knights. This isn't the kind of guy I was imagining at all!*

For the time being, we returned to Brunhild castle. Then, we took the group of Lestian knights toward the barracks of our own knight order. Some of them decided to stay as escorts for the visiting royalty, of course.

We entered the castle, and I was about to guide them, but…

"Eeek!!"

"Ohohohohhh…"

"Grandfather!" The incident kept repeating itself. Our maids didn't even have a chance. I was worried he'd end up causing an international incident, honestly.

I was sorely tempted to restrain him with **[Gravity]**, but…

"Oho… It's Touya. Good morning, y'know?" My sister… Karen, walked around the corner all of a sudden. In a flash of lightning speed, the former king of Lestia bolted toward her, hand groping its way toward her butt.

Before I could blink, however, the old man was on the ground, rolling in the opposite direction.

"What…" From my perspective, Karen's posture hadn't changed. She was clearly untouched. It was as if she hadn't moved. The dumbfounded old man stayed there on the floor, staring into space.

"Hey bro, who's this guy?"

"Huh, oh… He's the former king of the Lestia Knight Kingdom."

"Oh, gosh… He's certainly a lively old man, y'know?" I introduced Karen to our Lestian visitors, who were equally as surprised as I. Given that Karen was posing as my sister, that also technically made her royalty, too.

"Please forgive my sister, she can be a little… brash."

"No, goodness no! This was our fault from the beginning! I honestly think my grandfather needed something like that. A little divine punishment, ahaha." She had no idea how close to the truth she was. I kept my mouth shut, though. Her grandfather was lucky to only be slightly injured after trying to grope the ass of a literal god.

"But truly, you're amazing. Suppose I'd expect as much of His Highness' elder sister. This is the first time I've met a woman who can repel my grandfather's advan...ces... Erm... i-is there something on my face?"

Karen was staring intently at Hildegard. Her eyes were wide, as if staring into the poor girl's soul and searching for secrets. After a little while, Karen abruptly spoke up.

"You're in love, aren't you?"

"Wh-Huhwhat?!" Hildegard shrieked, shrinking back as crimson shot across her cheeks. Her composed expression was completely obliterated, replaced by a profusely sweating brow and panicked eyes.

"Wh-Whatever do you, uhm... mean?! L-Love?! Love?! HAHAHA! Ha! Don't be silly, ma'am!"

"Mfuhuhu... Love can never escape my gaze, y'know? Would you like me to give you some pointers? You should come to my room later, I'll teach you proper courtship etiquette." My dear older sister left for the dining room after leaving a weird passing comment. Hildegard was beet red, both hands over her face. I couldn't quite make out what she was muttering, either.

"Hey, uh, you okay?"

"Huh?! Yeah! HAHA! I'm great! I'm really, really great, actually. Thank you so much for asking, but I am great!" *Are you sure about that...? If you were any redder there'd be steam coming out of your ears.*

Still, if Karen had said she was in love, then she was in love. When the Goddess of Love said something about that, I'd be inclined to believe it. It seemed that in the end even female knights have the hearts of fair maidens. Her face turned so red after thinking about the guy she liked. He was a lucky one.

I was a little weirded out because she kept glancing at me now and then. She must've been embarrassed that I saw her in such a state.

"Anyhow… Princess Hildegard, and uh, former king… shall we be off?"

"A-Ah, uhm… please don't call me Hildegard. There's no need for such formality. I'd like it if… you called me Hilde. That's what I prefer to be called by those close to me…" The princess made a bashful request. I certainly didn't mind, since her name was a bit of a mouthful. With that, I decided to honor her request for my own convenience.

"Alrighty then. You'll be Hilde to me from now on."

"G-Great!"

"Ohohohohh…" Princess Hilde smiled broadly, but her grandfather just chuckled ominously in the background.

What's so funny, old man?!

"So then, what brings you both here?" Princess Hilde and her grandfather sat on a three-person couch in the castle's meeting room. I sat opposite them, hearing them out.

They'd informed me that they'd been traveling incognito, and didn't intend to give away their social status during the trip. Upon closer inspection, their armor didn't have the Lestian Royal Crest on it.

The former king was a great adventurer once, so he had contacts all over the place. Thanks to that, they arrived without a hitch. The guy sure was something.

From what I'd heard, they'd disguised themselves as commoners and went around fighting criminals... Kinda like Mito Komon from that one period drama show. I could almost imagine them facing down criminals with cries of "Do you know who this man is?! He's the great Galen, former king of the land!" and then they'd all be like "Ha-haaa!" or something... It probably wasn't that close to the show, though. Still, I didn't really have an issue with him delivering punishment to evildoers.

"Yes, we'd actually like to discuss the Yulong incident with you..." Hilde brought up the subject pretty quickly. I wasn't too surprised, all things considered.

The incident had involved several members of foreign countries, and Yulong had been spreading all kinds of baseless and inconsistent lies about what happened, so most nations that weren't involved had no idea about what had actually happened. That issue was mostly prevalent on the eastern side of the continent, as the western allies all knew the truth.

It was somewhat amusing that the west knew more about the situation at the east, given that it was an eastern situation to begin with.

The guild had been circulating the truth of the matter, but the facts did sound stranger than fiction. Beasts unaffected by magic, with complex regeneration abilities, and they appearing out of a tear in space? Nobody had ever heard of such a thing, so it was reasonable not to believe it.

I detailed exactly what had happened to the two of them, since there was no need to lie.

"Wow... So there really was an invasion by the Phrase creatures... So you're saying that Belfast, Regulus, Mismede, Refreese, Ramissh, and Lihnea were all fighting as one?"

"The Phrase are foes we couldn't have defeated if we weren't united. Just one of their Upper Constructs wiped Shenghai from the map in a single attack."

"What a frightful story… Do you think this could happen again, elsewhere?" The former king's worries were certainly justified. After all, a small group of Phrase had appeared in Lestia some time ago. I decided not to lie to these two, and gave them the honest truth of the matter.

"I don't think that anything like this will happen for a while, but there is still a real possibility this event could repeat itself elsewhere. It's for that reason that I've been preparing countermeasures."

"That's the Frame Gears, right? The giant warriors?" I was surprised they knew it by name, but at the same time I knew word would get out eventually.

I decided in this case it would be better to show rather than tell, so we moved to the western plain outside the castle. Along with their escorts, of course.

The former king, the princess, and the escorts were all taken by surprise as I warped them through my portal. I kept forgetting people weren't used to that. They were even more surprised when I used [Gate] to materialize a Black Knight in the field.

"This is one of my Frame Gears. I call it the Knight Baron. It's one of our primary weapons in combating the Phrase." The people in the area were absolutely speechless. I took out a radio from [Storage] and contacted Monica. She was sitting in the cockpit, of course.

"Alright, show them some motion. Don't mess around, though."

"As you command, Master." Monica started displaying various movements with the Frame Gear. She walked, ran, drew a weapon, thrust, and slashed.

"And these... Frame Gears... How many were deployed in Yulong?"

"Around two-hundred-and-fifty of them, including spare units. It was pretty close, given that there were around thirteen-thousand Phrase."

"Two-hundred-and... Wh-What does Brunhild intend to do with this military might?" The former king's eyes fell upon me, as if attempting to probe me for information. I couldn't really blame him. Anyone would suspect someone's intentions if they wielded this much power.

"You can believe me or not, but I do not intend on using this power to conquer. I would only use them in grave circumstances. Their first and foremost purpose is to fight the Phrase. I can promise you that even other members of the western alliance would not be wielding one of these unless a real crisis occurred."

"And how do you define a real crisis?"

"If a Behemoth were to emerge, or if we needed to rescue people from natural disasters. Those are crisis situations to me." I'd actually lent Frame Gears to a couple of allied nations for situations just like those. If they were saving lives, then obviously I'd let them make use of my power. I didn't charge them either, so it was a show of good faith on my part. My primary goal was to inspire confidence in foreign nations, to reassure them that I wasn't going to take over their homes. That being said, I'd make them compensate me if the Frame Gears were damaged fighting Behemoths or whatever.

"Then, as an example... if Lestia were to form an alliance with Brunhild, would we gain access to these Frame Gears as well?"

"If you were using them for honest situations and not war, then yes." They asked me if I was worried about foreign nations stealing the technology and reverse-engineering it. I challenged them to show me a place in the world that could do it. Not even my workshop could produce a Frame Gear from scratch. Unless a once-in-a-blue-moon genius like Doctor Babylon showed up, I had nothing to worry about.

They could disassemble a Frame Gear, but even then they'd be able to replicate the limbs at most. They wouldn't be able to distill the Ether Liquid, either. If a country actually did disassemble one of my Frame Gears to the point where it couldn't be put back together, I'd simply blacklist them from borrowing it anymore.

"The reason I came to Brunhild was to establish friendly relations. I can't formally propose an alliance without my son, though I'm sure he wouldn't reject it."

"I'd be happy to forge an alliance with Lestia, but I'd need to consult my other allies first." I didn't really expect there to be any objections, but formalities were still formalities. I was quite pleased with my image of Lestia so far. Being a Kingdom of Knights they seemed to be dutiful, honest, and noble people. This grope-happy old man was probably the only stain on that image so far.

I briefly wondered if the western alliance would have to change its name if Lestia joined. They were from the eastern part of the map, after all. Well, that was a minor detail, so I decided to worry about it later.

"Haaaaaah!!!"

"Hiyaaaaaah!!!" The two fighters halted inches before their wooden swords made contact with their enemy's body. Princess Hilde's sword rested itself at Yae's waist, while Yae's sword hovered just behind the nape of Hilde's neck. They were both extremely talented at swordplay.

"Alright. Match over." I'd volunteered to referee, so I used that power to end it there.

Hilde said she wanted to face my nation's greatest swordsman, so I decided Yae would be the best fit. After all, when it came to the art of the blade, she was even more adept than old man Yamagata.

Over the last year, I'd shown Yae countless websites and videos relating to traditional swordsmanship. She absorbed the info about as well as how a sponge absorbed water, and studied almost every day. Her style had really started to come into its own. Sure, her family's Kokonoe style left its mark on her, but she had evolved beyond it.

Still, the fact that Princess Hilde could fight Yae to a draw was astounding in itself.

The two of them lowered their weapons and breathed heavily.

"That was a very fun match. You truly have a wonderful knight, Your Highness."

"Hm? Ah, I am not one of his knights, I am not."

"Eh?" Hilde shook Yae's hand, but tilted her head in confusion at her words.

"I am betrothed to Touya-dono, I am."

"Er… excuse me?"

"Ah, she's my fiancee." I butted in to clarify, but Hilde suddenly stopped moving. *Huh? What's wrong?* She slowly turned toward me, almost creaking as she stared. I had no idea what was going on, but her eyes looked completely lifeless.

"Engaged… You're… engaged…?"

"Hm? Well, yeah… Wasn't there a big announcement about me marrying Lu and Yumina?"

"Yumina…? Lu…?" It felt like Hilde wanted to ask who they were. She didn't seem to recognize the names at all. I figured the news had yet to spread to the eastern side of the world or something.

"They are the princesses of Regulus and Belfast, they are. Like myself, they are both Touya's fiancees as well, they are."

"Whaaat?! H-He has three fiancees…?"

"Actually he has six, he does."

"SIX?!" Hilde was stunned into silence. *Hmm… I guess she's surprised. Even though polygamy's normal in this world, it's unusual for nobles or wealthy merchants to have two or three wives, and most outrageous members of royalty usually cap it off at five.*

Many merchants and nobles had wives, and then many concubines.

Apparently once a highborn man in this world took a wife, he'd have intimate relations with several women over the following years. But people like me with multiple marriage partners off the bat were considered rare.

"I… Well, I just… I didn't… expect that. Excuse me." Hilde muttered to herself, a little frown on her face. I waved my hand in front of her face, but she was completely lost in her own bubble.

"Looks like a job for Big Sis, y'know?!"

"Gah! Don't do that!" I jumped in surprise at the sudden voice.

Karen had appeared out of nowhere, striking a dramatic pose. Her breath was heavy, bated with excitement.

Geez, can this girl teleport or something?! Well, I guess she's a god rather than a girl… so she can just pop up as she pleases…

"Hey there, sweetheart. You're suffering from a case of one-sided unrequited love, y'know? And the target of that love is Touya, isn't it?"

"Eeep! Wh-What are you saying?! What?! Hahaha! WHAT?! That's so silly! H-How did you?! How did you guess like that?!" Karen pointed her finger over at Hilde, and the girl practically exploded into a deep blush. *What... Why's she freaking out? She can't... No... But we only met twice, no! No way! Please no... Don't say it!*

I pulled Karen off to the side and suddenly whispered to her.

"Wait just a second here... Are you using some kind of divine power here? Did you fire an invisible love beam at her or something?"

"Don't be so rude, Touya! I'd never interfere like that, y'know? That little girly over there has had love for you in her heart since the very beginning. Actually, I can see it and smell it. It's her first love. It's absolutely stunning, y'know?"

How is that so obvious to you?! Am I just slow or something? It's her first love, seriously?! So... What the hell do I do here? I had no idea what to do, and Hildegard was looking extremely awkward. Before I could think of something, Yae suddenly stepped in front of the poor girl. I reaaally hoped she wasn't going to fight her or something.

"Hilde-dono, do you love Touya-dono?"

"Eeep! I... No! Erm, that is to say... I didn't know he had a fiancee, especially not one so lovely as you, Yae. I... Please forgive me. I must be causing you grief."

"It is quite the contrary, it is. I know your feelings very well, I do. I was once in the same position as you." Hilde, who was looking at the floor in shame, slowly raised her head.

"When Touya-dono was first betrothed to Yumina-dono, I was simply his companion. I buried the affection I had deep within my heart, I did. But even so, both Touya-dono and Yumina-dono came to accept me."

"I see..."

"That is why I am comfortable with you joining our ranks as a fiancee, Hilde-dono."

"Excuse me?!" Both Hilde and I yelled the same thing at the same time. *How did this happen?! What is going on here?! I only took Sue as a fiancee recently, so isn't this a little soon for number seven?!*

"Right now, Touya's bridal limit is set to three more, it is. It has been decided that he will have nine wives in total."

"Nine?!" Hilde raised her voice in shock. *You're just sharing that now as well?! I didn't even agree!*

"Popular as ever, little bro… Your big sister's super proud of you, y'know?"

"Now hold it right there!" I glared at my idiotic sister, who had started wolf-whistling from the sidelines. *I'm glad somebody's seeing the funny side of all this!*

"S-S-So you're saying that he can only take on three more brides? That women after that would merely be his mistresses? I-If that's the case, then I gladly accept! I'll happily become the seventh, Yae!"

"Then I will have you introduced to the others later, I will. I am delighted that someone like you will be joining us."

"Thank you so much, Yae!" Princess Hilde grasped Yae's hand firmly.

Wait, what the hell just happened? Was my opinion voided entirely? Do I not matter?! This is bad… This is totally bad! It's gonna happen the same way it happened that time with Yumina and Lu. What can I even do? If I say something now, I'd just hurt her… Marriage is more than just love here, it also means deepening political and social ties. I guess us not knowing one another is fine to them because they're a society that nurtures love after political marriages, but... Agh! I don't know what to do, this is some weird upper-class custom or something...!

She is royalty, after all... Maybe it's a politically motivated decision? But no girl would choose to go marry someone she doesn't love...

The two girls quickly began chattering before my eyes. I was powerless to stop them, but luckily I didn't have to.

"Now hold your horses, I can't just allow this marriage!"

"Grandfather?!"

"Goodness me, what a situation this is..." The former king appeared as if from nowhere, jumping with outstretched hands and a serious expression on his face. *What is this, some kind of kabuki play?*

I'm getting a little worried this is gonna turn into a "If you want my granddaughter, you have to get through me!" kind of situation... That's not what I want at all!

"You would take the position of a Princess of Lestia so lightly...? Fight me, prove your worth!"

Bingo. Welp, guess there's no helping it. Still, this is a bit of a lucky situation; I can just lose on purpose. I don't intend to take Princess Hilde as my wife, not right now at least. She's cute, but I don't know the first thing about her!

Still... the former king is a Gold-rank adventurer. Despite his age, this might be a struggle, even if I don't throw the fight...

"You must honorably accept this duel. Show me your power, defeat me, and I'll accept you! Fight me now, Hilde!"

"Very well, Grandfather! I shall strike you down!"

Wait... What?!

"All opposed to the engagement between Touya and Princess Hildegard of Lestia, raise your hands now." Yumina spoke up, but nobody raised their hand.

"Then I happily accept Princess Hildegard as a kindred spirit. She, like us, will dutifully support Touya, striving to become good wives and mothers."

"Thank you so much! I'll work hard." Hilde shed a little tear as the other six stood around her and applauded. I had no idea what was happening.

There were eight people in the room. Myself, my fiancees, and Princess Hildegard. This was what they called a bridal conference, and the intention was to approve my engagement to Hilde. Though, for whatever reason, I was seated away from all the others.

"Come on, guys... You're seriously gonna ignore me here?" At my comment, Yumina turned and frowned.

"Do you dislike Princess Hilde?"

"Well, no. Don't see any reason to."

"Then you think she's unattractive?"

"Of course not! She's really pretty."

"Then her personality's at fault?"

"No. She's a hard worker and gives her all for her homeland. I'm really impressed, in all honesty."

"Then there's an issue with her heritage?"

"Nope, not that either. She's a princess like you and Lu."

"Then there's nothing to object."

"Ugh..." Yumina finished up her questioning and flashed me a grin. I looked over at Princess Hilde, only to find her blushing deeply and looking at the floor. It was true that I didn't have a reason to refuse her, but... I kind of had the feeling that if I gave in at this point, they'd walk all over me forever. I could barely stand up to one of them individually... Seven combined and I'd be their abusable puppet! Polygamy sounded like a man's dream at first, but I quickly found that if his brides joined forces, he'd be done for.

"...A-Are you all really okay with this?"

"If I wasn't, I'd have raised my hand."

"As far as we're concerned, you're the same as us. We see you as a good friend, and we'd love to have you in the family. We all came to love Touya in our own ways, as well..." Elze and Linze reassured Hilde. I wondered how they could speak so confidently about her, but it was probably Yumina's Mystic Eye. That would explain it.

Whenever Yumina used her Mystic Eye, she could read the 'aura' of a person. A person pure of heart would appear shining and gleaming to her, but a person with wicked intent would seem muddy and foul.

I didn't know all the details, but she couldn't read much beyond the surface intentions in their heart. In the end, Yumina told me that she judged based on the color she saw and her own intuition.

In other words, she knew things about people in a roundabout way. She could tell the difference between a bad person wearing a chivalrous disguise, and a good person who was trying to act rough. Yumina must have appraised Hilde in this way, or at least that was what I figured, but...

"This is definitely a good opportunity for us. Yumina and I are princesses, but we hail only from the west. Hilde is from the east, and after the Yulong incident, she's princess of the largest nation there... There's a frightful power in connecting the east and west." Lu muttered this and that about political workings. It felt a little dangerous, honestly.

Forging a strong alliance with Lestia would be handy, but I didn't want to just do this for political reasons.

"But, I mean…"

"Touya, you need to speak up for yourself. Have more confidence in yourself and your decisions. As your sister said, you're a popular man!"

"…Am I really that popular?"

"Of course you are! Everyone here loves you to pieces!" Sue's words made my cheeks burn scarlet. *Gah! I don't know if I'm happy or just embarrassed…! Ugh… Damn it, I'd rather not be so wishy-washy after so much time, but this is just how I am…*

I looked over at Princess Hilde, and her nervous eyes met with mine. I was a little worried, since it almost looked like she was going to cry.

"…Alright, then. If everyone's agreed, it's fine." Everyone suddenly gathered around Princess Hilde and cheered for her. As I listened to their shrill, girly laughter, I was once more reminded that I had no power against them. A twinge of unease set in when I thought about my future.

"Hey, Princess Hilde. What about your battle with the former king?"

"Just Hilde is fine, thank you. From now on I'm both your fiancee, and your first knight." Princess Hilde, or uh, just Hilde, turned to me with a smile.

"Very well then, Hilde. So, about that fight with the former king… Is there any chance you can beat him?"

"If you want my true thoughts, I don't think it's likely… The likelihood of me fighting and prevailing against my grandfather is around one in ten." Those were seriously low odds. It was about what I'd expected, though. The old man must've been powerful. Still, one chance in ten was still a chance.

"And… the times I have won against him, I must say it wasn't due to my skills. It was just a case of me getting lucky…"

"Ha… So you're saying your victory is a matter of coincidence, then?"

"Y-Yes…" *Come on, Sue. Don't just say it like that. She looks depressed enough as it is!*

On the contrary, I thought perhaps her grandfather might end up being taken off-guard. If he doesn't take her seriously enough, she could use that to her advantage and come out on top.

The weapon for the duel was to be a sword, and it would be only a test of physical prowess. No magic was to be allowed.

"Touya-dono… Is there not something we can do?"

"Hm… Well, we could always lace Hilde's weapon with some kind of blinding poison, or make the hilt of his sword detonate or something… Or maybe I could just enchant Hilde's weapons and armor to have a ton of buffed up effects?"

"A-A victory like that would be rather… hollow, and a-against the code of chivalry." *I mean, I guess… but there's a lot of ways we could easily win here. The rules said magic couldn't be directly employed during the duel, so it's not technically cheating! Heheheheh…*

"You're making a wicked face again, you are."

"…You're probably coming up with something cruel and underhanded, aren't you? I don't know if that's a good thing."

"I-I'm a tad concerned…" *Don't be mean! I'm not thinking of anything wicked or underhanded, I promise!*

Not this time, at least.

The moment the match started, the former king cornered Hilde. She was forced into the corner, but still managed to think on her feet, parrying his wooden sword and batting it away from her.

"What's wrong, Granddaughter?! Are your feelings for the grand duke so pitiful that you'd falter here?!"

"...I believe in Touya! If I move as he instructs, then I shall surely win!"

"As he instructs?! Show me, then!" The speed of his attacks increased, striking Hilde over and over in an unstoppable barrage. The girl's defenses slowly started to crumble. She blocked his hits with a shield, but each strike caused vibrations against her arm. If that kept up, then her movements would end up being hindered.

The battle was being held in the underground arena. The audience was just myself and my fiancees. I had the escorts wait outside.

Hilde defended to the best of her ability. I told her to focus on defending and keep her eyes wide for a vital opening. With that, she'd be able to end the fight in a single shot.

Hilde smacked his wooden sword aside using her shield and created some room between them both. She was clearly running out of energy. Her breathing was ragged and unsteady.

On the other hand, the old man looked like he had life in him yet. A small smile painted his face.

"Hmph... He is strong, he is. His style is violent and unrefined, like a whirlwind. If Hilde-dono is a strong person, then he is truly a monster. He employs his weapon as a fearsome storm that favors brutality over technique, he does."

"But she's withstanding it pretty damn well. I think they're matching up great."

"That's just because she's solely focused on defense right now. She can't win if she keeps going as she is. Even if she focuses on her defenses, they'll eventually crumble. That's when she'll lose." Yae, Elze, and Lu... The three main fighters of my entourage offered their professional insights. I was especially amazed by how steadfast Lu had become recently. It was hard to believe that she was the one who was cowering in fear during the coup. It was possible that she was just in shock at the time, though.

She still wasn't quite up to the level of Yae or Elze, but she was definitely skilled. She ended up wielding her weapons in a way that combined my and Yae's fighting techniques, so she was mostly self-trained.

"It should be any time now... I hope she doesn't miss the opening."

"But will the former king actually leave an opening? He's powerful, and she's still an opponent he's taking seriously in the end..."

"He won't make an opening. Heheheh... I'm going to make the opening." I disregarded the confused Yumina and began to focus my magic. I'd browsed the internet for a convenient video, and now it was time to put it into action.

The former king charged toward Hilde, clearly intent on landing the final blow. That was my chance! I used **[Mirage]** to project an image of something about two meters behind Hilde.

"Whuh!" The former king's eyes shot open wide and he suddenly stopped moving. Hilde had no idea what had happened, but she took her chance. She smacked her training sword against her grandfather's body with all her might.

"Ghaugh!!!" If that had been a real sword, the hit would've split him in two. With that, the old man collapsed and fell on the ground. I'd done it!

"...Touya."

"Yeah?"

"...Who was that woman behind Hilde? The one wearing a... string-like bikini that appeared for a split second." A lewdly-posed pinup model clad in a teeny tiny micro-bikini was currently on my phone's display. I had no idea who she was, but her outfit was seriously risque. She had tanned skin, gorgeous eyes, and a voluptuous body.

"I did it! It's my victory! Oh, Touya, I did it! I won!" Hilde looked positively overjoyed, so I waved over to her. My other fiancees were smiling too, but I could hear their low, terrifying mutters.

"...That was a convenient opening..."

"Men are the worst..."

"I'll handle it, Sis..."

"H-Her chest was pretty big..."

"...Is that the kind of swimsuit you prefer?"

"Hm? Where are you going, Touya?" Everyone except Sue looked at me with dark eyes. I definitely couldn't stick around after employing one of the Thirty-Six Stratagems! I hopped down from the audience stands and walked over to congratulate Hilde. I felt piercing gazes digging into my back, but I didn't turn around.

"Touya, I really won! I can marry you!" Hilde didn't seem to think too hard about her grandfather's suspicious loss. She was simply celebrating as the old man groaned and grumbled on the floor.

"You've done well to defeat me... But know this... the second and third times you come at me, I will not make it so simple... This isn't even... my final form!"

"...Geez, what are you, a JRPG Archfiend...?" I cast recovery magic on the former king. Honestly, it was amazing to me that *this guy* was the king of a noble knightly society. Though, I had heard he was adopted by the generation before him... so that kind of explained why he didn't have the traditional knightly image.

The former king rose to his feet and turned to Hilde, apparently completely healed and recovered already.

"I know now the faults in my maturity. A loss is indeed a loss. Your resolve is clear as day to me, my dear. Thus, you may marry freely. ...As for the boy, I've no complaints either. From here on, you are no longer a knight of Lestia, so ensure you become a proud knight of Brunhild."

"Grandfather..."

"Touya, son... My granddaughter is only talented with a blade, but I entrust her to you until the end of time."

"...I understand, sir. I'll look after her." The former king bowed his head to me.

"A-Also... who was that pretty little number in the swimsuit?! Let me see her again! Even if only one more time, allow me to burn her voluptuous form into my mind!"

"...Swimsuit?"

"A-Ah... Sir, if uhm... If you'd bear with me a moment, then sure. I can't do it right here, so if we can just go to another room..."

"Ohoho, no problem! Hilde, you go with the others. They'll take care of you, I'm sure. Touya, Touya! Let's go!" The former king grabbed me by the arm and started dragging me off. I was kind of surprised he hadn't complained yet about the opening being unfair...

but part of me wondered if he was actually going to lose on purpose anyway.

In the end, he convinced me to use [**Drawing**] to print out a ton of pinup swimsuit model pictures for him to take home. I really wondered where his perverted powers came from…

I returned to my room, exhausted, only to find everyone except Sue and Hilde waiting for me. They violently interrogated me for a while, asking me about my preferences in women. They asked questions about whether bigger boobs were better, whether I preferred slim, toned women, or if I would prefer it if they changed their regular outfits for more risque and naughty versions.

In the end, I bowed down on the ground and begged for them to stop. Mostly because they suddenly proposed that they should all get micro-bikinis. I definitely couldn't allow them to do that, it would've been way too much.

…It might've been nice to see, though.

A few days later, I took our Lestian guests through a [**Gate**] back to their kingdom.

I was guided to their royal palace, and finally met up with the Knight King, Reid Yunas Lestia. Though I had the former king's blessing, I thought it prudent to come here and explain the situation myself.

I thought things were moving a little fast, but I was in too deep to rely on common sense. I wondered if he was more like me, or more like Hilde's grandfather. … I wondered if he'd end up being a weird old pervert like the former king.

"Hm… It may be a tad late for me to say this, but my father's way of doing things is certainly a little wild. All in all, I have no objections toward Hilde's marriage. Grand Duke Touya, I must commend you for taking on such a… rough girl as Hilde. She's certainly tomboyish in her pursuits, but I'm glad she's to your liking. We're indebted to you, really."

"I agree, thank you for accepting her. I'm proud of you, Hilde. You'll surely find happiness…"

"Congratulations, Hilde. Please, Grand Duke, take care of my little sister."

Wow… These guys, are uh… very proper. The king, the queen, and the prince… are all good people. That wacky old man really threw me for a loop! I thought these guys would be just as bad as he was, but they're actually pretty normal.

Or maybe it's because they were around this guy… He's a prime example of how not to behave.

They all seemed like kind and gentle people, so I was pleased. The king seemed to be around fifty years old. His hair was dark brown and cut short and his mustache had some gray hairs in it here and there. I had the feeling he was probably a popular guy in his youth.

Queen Esther looked to be in her mid-forties. She had a gentle aura about her, similar to Cecile's. The woman was noble and beautiful; she'd likely been the same way all her life. She seemed very motherly to me.

Hilde's older brother, Prince Reinhard, certainly looked the part. He was in his mid-twenties and had golden-blond hair like his sister. They'd likely inherited it from their mother. As much as I hated to admit it, the guy was really handsome, too… I heard he was engaged, as well. From what I could understand he was dignified, skilled with a blade, and quick-witted. He was basically an ideal candidate to be the next king.

"Father, Mother, Brother... I promise to find my own happiness!" Hilde shed tears of joy and pulled her mother into an embrace. It was a beautiful scene to watch, but I couldn't help but feel out of place. Here was a happy, loving family, and I was just kind of standing there.

"In truth, ahem... there's actually a reason I'm content to move your engagement forward. I intend to abdicate the throne to Reinhard... but there's a small issue with our ceremonial blade."

"Hm? What's that?"

"Ah, it's a holy sword that has been in our royal family for generations. It's the Holy Sword Lestia. It is the blade that bestowed its name to our country, and is very much the symbol of our royal line." As I heard Hilde's explanation, a knight entered the room and handed a long wooden box to the king.

The Knight King uttered a quiet spell, and I heard a clicking sound as the box unlocked. I actually heard the hiss of air rushing out, as well. It was a goddamn airtight sealed container! The box finally opened to reveal a beautiful sword.

It was a broadsword adorned with silver and gold. Alongside it was a magnificent and ornate sheath. It was definitely something one could easily call a king's sword.

"Oh, I see..." I frowned a little upon seeing the problem. The dazzling blade was snapped in half, split at the midpoint. It was completely ruined.

"This is Holy Sword Lestia. It's only used for ceremonial purposes, or if our nation is at war... Otherwise it's kept sealed. The last time it was used was during Hilde's formal initiation as a knight, three years ago."

"Once I decided to abdicate my throne to Reinhard, I removed the seal in order to prepare for his ceremony… but the sword was like this. I've no idea why the blade is broken… What I do know is that the ceremony cannot be performed like this. I was concerned about it all and was thinking of making an imitation sword as a last resort, but then… I heard of you from Hilde, Grand Duke." The Knight King unsheathed the blade at his waist, holding it gently in his hands. It was the sword I'd given to Hilde.

"Aye, we thought a man who could make a sword as glorious as this would surely be able to repair Lestia. That's why I traveled to Brunhild on my son's behalf. Though I must confess, I had personal interest in you, Touya. I wanted to know the kind of man my little Hilde had been dreaming of. I wished to judge your character."

"G-Grandfather…?"

"Over the past few months, whenever Hilde spoke, it was only about you, Grand Duke. She would wistfully sigh and look at the sword you gave to her. She thought we wouldn't notice, but how could I ignore the fact that she would always ask roving merchants about Brunhild?"

"You too, Brother?!" I cast a sidelong glance toward the flustered Hilde, but was more interested in the sword. It was… definitely old. What looked like ancient lettering was engraved into the blade itself. There was also a crystal embedded in the hilt.

"Mind if I hold it?"

"Go ahead." I gripped the broken blade by the hilt, taking a good look at it. I could almost feel some residual magic inside of it.

"Was this sword enchanted with a special effect?"

"Ha, you're quite the discerning one. I'm amazed you could tell just by looking. The sword has a regenerative effect on its wielder.

135

It patches up minor injuries, and even causes grievous wounds to regenerate."

I see... So I guess this thing's imbued with [**Healing**] *or something. Or was, rather... As it stands, the effect isn't triggering.*

"The best blacksmith in Lestia has also found himself unable to do a thing. I was told that the sword's material was something completely unknown to him. The regeneration ability is gone now, too... I fear that it's completely ruined..."

"What do these letters say?"

"Ah, I have no idea. There was nothing mentioned about it in our family history. The language seems to be the one used by the ancient civilization, Partheno."

Huh... Guess there's one way to find out!

"[**Reading**]: **Ancient Partheno Language.**" I had a handy Null spell, though this one hadn't seen use for a while. It allowed me to read any language, so long as I knew what the language was to begin with.

"What the..." My shoulders slumped, drained of energy. I was completely bamboozled. The lettering on the blade was a signature. The kind of thing someone carved into their work to prove it was theirs. And, with [**Reading**], I was able to see what it was. I had no idea what I expected, but it wasn't this.

"Designed by Regina Babylon."

Why did it have to be here? Why was that no-good doctor even in the business of making swords? I briefly pondered if this was fate, but… as far as she was concerned, I had no idea what was engineered and what wasn't.

"Is something wrong, Touya?"

"N-No, it's… just… This sword was made by the same person who made the Frame Gears…"

"What?!" The former king went wide-eyed. I had no idea why this sword was here, nor did I expect to find it… Though it had me wondering if this wasn't more of a Horny Sword than a Holy Sword, given that pervy doctor's inclinations.

"…It's been over five-thousand years, so it's possible the magical power's just drained. You've had it sealed all this time, right? Only using it now and then for ceremonies? It's possible it's been weakening little by little because it's been cut off from the residual magic in the air." I was thinking that if it had been cut off from magic and weakened, magic might've been what kept it intact. It definitely wouldn't have much time to absorb any magic if it only kept coming out briefly now and then. There was really no wonder why it snapped just like that.

It was kind of like an animal that didn't get much food every day, and slowly lost weight until it died.

"F-Five-thousand years…? But… this is the blade of our royal founder. I don't believe our history stretches back that far."

"When was Lestia founded?"

"Around three-hundred years ago… Two-hundred-and-ninety-one, if I'm to be precise. It was said that our founder wielded Lestia, used its power to unify the squabbling tribes in the area, and created the Knight Kingdom of Lestia."

...I think I've got it. What the prince said just now... It would all make sense. No, it's not that it would make sense; it's pretty much definitely what happened. I've seen this situation before! I know what it is! This thing definitely fell down from the storehouse! Then, a wandering knight must have picked it up... And then he used its power to end the warring in the region... and ultimately founded the Knight Kingdom of Lestia. That's pretty damn amazing.

Honestly, the gynoid in charge of the storehouse had been clumsy and irritating, so she wound up causing me a lot of trouble. But I figured this was an example of it turning out in a positive way. In the end, what mattered was how the item was used.

"Well, I'll be able to repair it. There shouldn't be an issue. I'll be able to re-apply the enchantment, too."

I cast [**Modeling**] on it and joined it back together. The previous enchantment vanished due to that, but I'd easily be able to re-apply the effect. I also increased the magical reserve that the weapon held. So long as they didn't seal it back in that box, they wouldn't have to worry about it running out.

"Oooh!"

"There we go. It's back to normal."

"Thank you. Now we can proceed with the ceremony as usual. We're in your debt." The king took the Holy Sword in his right hand, and sliced at his own left arm. Blood flowed from the wound, but the cut closed almost immediately.

"It works as it did before... Actually, it feels a little faster."

Oh boy... did I accidentally give it a stronger effect? The magic should run out faster if that happens... Still, it's better this way, honestly.

The sword would absorb magic from the air and slowly build it up over time, then use that magic to preserve itself and heal its owner, but naturally that would slowly deplete the reserve.

But that was fine, because the weapon would just continue to recover that reserve through the air. It was a slow process that accumulated over time. Ideally you wouldn't want to use it all up in one go, or the sword wouldn't have a special function for a while.

It could probably only heal to the equivalent of ten [**Cure Heal**] uses, or five [**Mega Heal**] uses… so it wasn't perfect, but it was pretty good in a pinch. Still, I'd increased its magic pool so it could store a bit more than before, so I figured it wouldn't be an issue.

Holy Sword Lestia as it was before wasn't exactly perfect either, so this would be fine. Infinite free healing simply wasn't feasible.

Or, well… maybe it wasn't… I felt like I could probably make something like that if I put my mind to it. Worst-case scenario, I'd end up creating something like that immortality gem I'd encountered in Eashen… I decided not to think about it. A person may as well discard their humanity if they had an item that prevented them from dying.

"It may be a little different to how it was before, sorry…"

"No, no… You've done us a great service. Thank you so very much." The king sheathed the sword, but he didn't put it in the sealed box this time. He didn't have to go that far, though. I ended up explaining to him that so long as he exposed it to fresh air for a full day every year, then it'd be okay. In the end, he agreed that the box seal would be undone once a year, on the anniversary of the country's founding.

After that, it was time to celebrate the prince's ascension to the throne. I decided to gift him a phrasium blade. I'd given one to the former king, Hilde, and the king... but back then I didn't know there was a prince.

I'd designed it in the same shape as Lestia's. It was made to be light, sharp, and indestructible. It was the perfect blade for battle. It wouldn't be good for training matches or duels, though. It was way too sharp. If a sword clashed with it, the weaker blade would surely shatter.

"It's a wonderful gift. In truth, my son was a little envious of us for our beautiful blades, but now his is the most wonderful of all... I'm quite pleased, all in all. It's a wonderful gift for him, thank you." I was happy that he was happy. He was going to be my brother-in-law, so I'd hoped to maintain good relations.

A few days later, a new king was crowned in Lestia. Along with his ascension, the engagement of First Princess Hildegard was announced. Thus, Hilde formally became my fiancee.

"It's getting colder, huh…"

Brunhild was entering its winter season. It wasn't half as cold as the Kingdom of Elfrau was when I'd visited, but it was still quite bad. It looked like snow was due, too.

"Do we have sufficient countermeasures to stave off the cold?"

"All the houses in Brunhild have fireplaces. We have ample stores of firewood, too. If anything, our concern should be preventing fires." That was true. We formed a small fire brigade just in cases any places got lit up. Also, there was a device much like a pump so fires could be extinguished quickly. Kousaka was definitely thorough in his approach, so it was good to have him around. It seemed the water from the town's canal would be our primary method of opposing fire. For now, having them go on occasional patrols would be enough. Maybe I'd equip them with some claves they could slap together to alert others or something.

After finishing my formal affairs, I headed to the courtyard training grounds. Hilde and Rebecca were both in the midst of a duel.

After she was officially announced as my fiancee, Hilde had come to live in my castle.

In all honesty, I didn't expect her to come live with me until the wedding. Fiancee or not, she was still the princess of another nation, and had national duties.

Unlike Yumina, who seemed to take a while to settle with me, Lu and Hilde seemed to have settled in relatively quickly. They were right at home. As you might expect, Sue was the only one who didn't live with me. She still stayed over two nights a week, though.

Obviously, she didn't sleep in my room either. She mostly stayed with Yumina. Though I'd noticed she stayed with Renne some nights.

I didn't mind her staying overnight, but she really had to stop sneaking into my room in order to wake me up. It was a little much to be woken up twice a week by a little girl's body slamming into me.

As I winced, recalling the pain, Hilde wandered over toward me.

"Touya!"

"Nice job, Hilde." I cast **[Refresh]** and restored all of her fatigue. Whenever she had time, she'd come to train here against my soldiers. I wouldn't have expected anything less from a knight.

Hilde wasn't wearing the Lestian armor that she wore when we first met, though. Instead, she had light armor of Brunhild's design on. Despite the fact that she was a knight, she didn't belong to my country's knight order. She herself said she wasn't a knight of Brunhild, but my own personal knight... I knew for a fact that Commander Lain felt a little awkward having someone so close to me fighting alongside them.

"Are you off somewhere?"

"I'm heading to the guild. Brunhild's branch finally opened up, so I'm gonna check it out."

"Ooh... May I come with you?"

"Don't see why not. Let's go." Having her come with me and see the town was on the agenda, so this was handy. I wanted her to get used to Brunhild sooner rather than later.

I left the castle with Hilde. On our way into town, we passed a bunch of excited children who didn't seem to care at all about the cold.

"Heeey, Milord! Nice to see ya!"

"Nice to see ya, Milooord!"

"Ah, yeah... Good to see you. Don't wander off too far, now."

"Ohkaaay!" The cheery kids ran off toward the fields. I'd been considering it for a while, but I definitely needed to make a school. Kids that could read and write, and learn other skills, would be useful to have in the country. Then again, I didn't have any teachers.

We didn't have too many talented people amongst the general population...

"The children are happy... That's good, it makes me happy too."

"Yeah... We managed to build up the country without needing them to chip in and work. That's a good thing, really." Brunhild could be considered a fairly well-off country. We didn't have anything in the way of poverty, and most people had jobs, but we also didn't really have anything in the way of industry... Unless you counted bicycle production. I was doing some experiments with trade, agriculture, and manufacturing, but it was nothing concrete just yet.

I'd asked Flora to improve several types of seed for me, so I wanted to kick off more agricultural production, but... our territory wasn't all that vast or wide, so we were a little limited in our operations.

As I pondered such things, we finally arrived at our destination, Brunhild's guild hall. The place was already a little crowded. It seemed that the guild was operating like any other.

I pulled a hood over my head and went inside. The crowd was pretty noisy, come to think of it. The quest board had a ton of people in front of it checking out all the different posts. Part of me missed the atmosphere. I'd completely changed my life since I first arrived in this world.

Hilde kept looking around restlessly. I wondered if this was the first time she'd been in a guild hall.

"Welcome! Are you a newcomer?"

"Ah, no… I just came to visit. Is the manager in?" I gave a vague answer to the cat-eared receptionist and quietly flashed her my card. There were only two Golds on the continent, after all.

"Wh…! W-Wow… A-Ah… Please wait just a moment!" The flustered catgirl stumbled off up the stairs while her colleagues looked on in confusion. I briefly caught the glance of a few adventurers, but they very quickly returned their gazes to the quest listings. A few were glancing at Hilde, but that wasn't too surprising. She stuck out like a sore thumb, after all.

After a while, the cat-eared girl came down and spoke in a low whisper.

"I'll take you to see the manager now… Y-Your Highness…!" The girl led me off up the stairs, and we passed through to the back room. There, someone I knew quite well was waiting on me.

"Huh? You're the manager here, Relisha?" Relisha, the elven guildmaster, stood there and smiled at me. She was supposed to be one of the great guildmasters of the west. I wondered if she'd been demoted or something.

"No, not quite. A guildmaster can choose which guild branch becomes their home base, but I hadn't decided. However, after establishing the Brunhild branch, I finally made my choice."

"Oh, so that's how it is…" I pulled down my hood and took a seat. The room I was in was surprisingly gaudy, with several documents and books adorned the place, neatly organized on shelves. There were various magically-charged items dotted around, too. Guildmasters certainly lived interesting lives.

"Ah, Grand Duke... I've been informed you're engaged to the Lestian princess. Please accept my congratulations."

"Ah... Thank you."

"A-Ah! Thank you so much!" *Hilde... That was loud.* She squirmed in embarrassment, completely oblivious to my thoughts as I looked at her.

"On to other matters, the Yulong incident troubles me greatly. The guild branch there was almost completely wiped out. The survivors were gravely wounded. It will take a considerable amount of time, but we will rebuild. Adventurers are necessary in a place with shattered morale." As I'd expected, the effects of the incident were catastrophic. The information on the Phrase had been sent to the other guildmasters, but not the individual hall staff. Had they known, they may have found some way to escape.

"Are there any new reports of Phrase activity?"

"None at all, no. Do you believe it could happen again, Your Highness?"

"I don't think it's over, but I can't tell you when it'll happen again. Tomorrow? A year? Ten years? I just can't say." Relisha frowned slightly, placing a hand to her chin as if deep in thought.

"For now, we can continue to spread the warnings. I hope the same thing doesn't happen in Yulong, though... Especially not after we rebuild." Relisha chuckled faintly, as if she were telling a joke. Still, it was undeniable that the possibility of disaster was ever present. I saw the tear in reality form back in Yulong. There wasn't any guarantee it wouldn't open once more.

The towns and buildings themselves weren't especially damaged, since the Phrase went after living targets exclusively, but many people didn't want to live there simply because of the fact that a genocide had occurred.

The people of Yulong became refugees, having no choice but to escape to neighboring nations. Some of them became thieves and brigands, while others earned money defeating them... The lives of many were changed by the incident.

"There are still many in Yulong who believe the invasion was your work, Grand Duke. But nobody outside of that country believes in it, I can assure you. The refugees who leave always end up learning the truth, as well. The more people they meet, the fewer lies they believe. I'm certain the stories won't persist much longer."

"They can say whatever they want, honestly. I'm just about done with Yulong."

"They've been rallying people lately with catchphrases and slogans like 'Never forgive, never forget.' It's entirely possible they may cause trouble for you down the line."

"Then I'll crush whoever's rallying them should it come to that. I'm not a wimp, so if someone causes me trouble, then I'll squash them. Peace begets peace, and violence breeds violence." I had no choice but to take that stance. I sympathized with Yulong, but this was another matter entirely. I didn't want anything to do with their lies.

"We'll spread such a message from our guilds, then. Something along the lines of 'The grand duke of Brunhild is a benevolent man, but he will surely strike down anyone that opposes his nation.' Something to that effect." I figured that'd be enough. Though I didn't want to be exaggerated out of context too much... Still, there was nothing I could do. I decided to change the subject.

"How's the guild going?"

"Well, it's going. We're employing plenty of people for general quests, and missions to kill monsters are coming in from Belfast and Regulus. The only real issue is there aren't any high-tier missions available... Though, I suppose that's a testament to how peaceful Brunhild is, no?" There weren't any magic beasts around or anything, and I'd cleared out all the brigands. The quests here wouldn't be fulfilling for people who wanted to earn a lot at once, since it was mostly small stuff.

Just then, I heard some rowdy voices from downstairs. I wondered what it could be. I asked Relisha, and she told me that disputes were regular in guild halls, and fights were just a part of life here.

I wasn't too surprised. After all, I'd been involved in a few conflicts like that myself.

"Hey, twerp. This isn't a place you can just stroll into, got it?"

"Come on, now. Don't you think you're just talking tough because you have a woman with you?"

"Shut it. I'll teach you how to be a *real* adventurer. Your wallet can be my payment."

...The situation didn't exactly sound amicable.

Guilds typically didn't interfere in disputes between adventurers. So long as there was no damage to the property, it wasn't their business.

If people scuffled, they typically took it outside anyway. That was one of the reasons the guild was built with a wide area in front of it.

Eventually we heard loud footsteps that grew fainter as people went outside. I figured they must've been asked to leave by the staff.

"Oh, seems they've taken it outside," Relisha muttered to herself as she peeked out the window.

That reminded me of my own experience too. I'd once been told to take it outside. Back then they'd intended to humiliate me in front of the town, rather than just the guild, but they were the ones who ended up humiliated.

"Hmph… Aren't they ashamed of ganging up on one person like that…? It's a woman, as well…" Hilde peeked out the window. She seemed rather interested as well.

"She seems stronger than them, though. See? She beat a bunch already."

"Incredible. She must be strong to heft that axe around… She's certainly light-footed as well. It looks like she might just be naturally talented, since she's not moving like she has formal training… Her clothes are strange, as well…"

"I believe that's the traditional garb of the Rauli tribe, from the Sea of Trees. I never expected to see one of them out here…"

Huh…? What'd they say just now…? The Rauli Tribe… Why does that ring a bell?

I peeked out from another window and saw four men on the ground. A tanned woman was fighting a fifth.

What?! That girl!

"Touya?" Ignoring Hilde, I darted out of the room, bolted past reception, and ran outside. I made it there just in time to see the girl kick the last man hard in the side of the face.

The onlookers cheered as the girl looked down on her attackers.

Suddenly, her eyes fell upon me. As I'd expected, it was her. She was the granddaughter of the Rauli tribe chief, and the girl who bit me way back when. Her name was Pam, if I recalled correctly.

"… Found you."

Huh? Did she just speak? I didn't know she could speak the common tongue.

My thoughts were interrupted by Pam suddenly charging over and embracing me. She bowled me over and started rubbing her cheek against mine.

W-Wait a second now! The girl was wearing something like a hide mantle, but she only had a chest wrap and a loincloth covering her breasts and nether region respectively. She was… hitting against me, in various ways. They were definitely as big as I remembered.

"Wh-What are you doing?!" I looked toward the guild's entrance and saw Hilde standing there, red in the face. She was fidgeting like crazy.

…This feels dangerous. Oh geez… Yep, this is a familiar sensation…

"What are you doing?! Get off Touya!"

"Who you? This Pam's lover. Pam am having baby with him."

"Wh-Wh-Wh-What?!" Hilde's cheeks grew redder than beets.

What the hell is going on here?! I don't understand! Someone explain the situation, damn it!

"I can't allow this."

"Why? If child born from Touya and Pam is girl, our tribe raises. If child is boy, you raise."

Yumina simply replied with a sigh and a shake of her head.

"I'm sorry, but you aren't suited to become Touya's wife. You really need to leave."

"Pam doesn't wish to be bride. Just having Touya's seed is good. With Touya's seed, I make strongest baby to become queen of Sea of Trees." Well, her intentions were certainly plain and simple. We'd been talking in circles for hours. Pam had left the Sea of Trees in order to find me. She'd learned the common tongue during the trip, so it seemed she was smarter than I'd initially given her credit for.

After the fuss in the guild, a bridal conference was called. The theme of the meeting was "Can Pam be accepted?"

"Pam don't know why you guys have problem."

"You're more than free to want a baby, Pam, but it's another matter entirely if it's Touya's child as well. You'd choose the prosperity of your people over Touya's happiness. A person like that can't be allowed to have his baby." Yumina glared down at Pam with a tremendously imposing force behind her words. In all honesty, she scared me a bit too.

"...The baby doesn't have to be Touya's, does it? It doesn't need to be him if you want a strong child. Just go sleep around with some strong men, I'm sure one of them will take hold." Linze let loose some bitter words as well. She seemed to be fully behind Yumina's stance here.

"Cannot. Pam has given Touya the Oathbite. That mean Touya is Pam's."

"How utterly selfish! There's no way Touya would acknowledge something so stupid!" Hilde stood up in her chair and yelled over at Pam. Sounded like that bite Pam had given me a while ago was the equivalent of a promise in their culture. Something like 'I've marked this guy as mine, so back off.'

Their culture really didn't care about men or their personal circumstances. It was entirely female-dominated. They were pretty similar to the traditional idea of the Amazons.

"Let us begin from the start, yes? Why do you wish to bear Touya-dono's child? There must surely be more than your simple reason, there must." Yae took a more gentle approach in quizzing Pam, to which the brown-skinned girl replied by frowning and muttering.

"We tribe of war... But we do not attack others, except for making child. We fight to protect home, but not to attack others. Still, lately many tribes attack us stronger and harder. Strong blood needed so we can stay in Sea of Trees. Also to win during the pruning."

"Hm...? What's the pruning?" Sue tilted her head slightly and asked a question. As far as I understood it, pruning was when you cut off troublesome branches and leaves from trees in order to make it look better or help fruits grow.

"The Pruning is war between tribes of Sea of Trees. Every ten years, warriors from every tribe comes battle to decide which tribe is strongest. Winning tribe becomes Tribe of the Treelord and can make one law in Sea of Trees."

Every ten years, huh... Well, that sounds interesting. I guess the winning tribe can establish a law to make it easier for his tribe and harder on the others.

"A law? So can you pick and choose anything? What if you wanted to make a law to expel a tribe or something?" Elze took the words right out of my mouth. I wondered if you could make a law like 'Tribe A must pledge obedience to Tribe B' or something like that. I doubted you could make a dumb law like 'Give me a hundred more laws,' though.

In classic stories involving situations with one wish, there's usually a rule against wishing for more wishes.

"If allowed by Great Wishing Tree, yes. If it does not dishonor tribe, then any law."

"Great... Wishing Tree?"

"Is guardian deity of us. Grants all tribes spirit's blessing and protection."

...Like one of those trees you tie talismans to? Still, I kinda wonder what she means by spirits. Hopefully nothing like the one that rampaged around in Ramissh... If there's a wishing tree like that, I wonder... Does the Sea of Trees have a forest spirit?

From what I understood, spirits were benign for the most part. In the case of the one at Ramissh, it went berserk due to being sealed underground for centuries. Plus, it was kind of an asshole after it fused with Ramirez and gained his negativity.

The people from the Sea of Trees lived their lives worshiping this wishing tree and lived according to a spiritual creed. In a way, they were similar to the people of Ramissh.

"Rauli tribe loses in Pruning for last seventy years now. Other tribes take in new blood. Strong blood. Pam and Touya's baby will win Pruning. Restore honor and glory. If Pam do nothing, Rauli tribe destroyed by Balm tribe soon."

"The Balm tribe? They're another tribe in the Sea of Trees, then?"

"Yes. Is tribe that says women less good than men. They steal woman from other tribes, fill seed, make many babies. If baby boy, raise as warrior. If baby girl, cast out mother and child."

That's not all that different from the Rauli tribe, though... Just a reversal of roles, honestly. Not that I'm saying either is right, it's quite awful.

There seemed to be a deep hate between the male-dominated tribe, Balm, and the female-dominated tribe, Rauli. Given their creeds, there could probably never be peace between the two.

Both tribes were strong enough to keep the other in check, but the arrival of the Spider Phrase caused catastrophic damage to the Rauli people. The warriors that were to represent the tribe in the pruning ended up dying. Because of that, they were sitting ducks for the Balm tribe to pick away at.

"We given up on winning next Pruning. Only hope that Balm does not win and become Tribe of the Treelord. But Pam and Touya's child can win next Pruning, and we become Tribe of the Treelord." That was certainly a long-term plan. Still, after hearing her circumstances, I couldn't accept. I didn't want her to give birth to my daughter just to make the girl fight. That would be horrible.

"When's the next Pruning?"

"One month. We fight. Tribe brings great shame if not participating. We will lose. Pam not fight because Pam is here. Pruning has five tribe champions fight other tribe's five champions. If unlucky, you die." That sounded terribly dangerous. From what I had heard, the Pruning followed a simple set of rules. It was similar to a five-versus-five tournament. It was beginning to sound more and more like a military event than anything else.

"Hm..."

"Yumina?" Yumina was deep in thought as Lu tried calling out to her.

"What kind of law will the Balm tribe add if they win this Pruning?"

"Likely some law that drives Rauli tribe to edge of Sea of Trees. Bad hunt, bad soil. Hard to live. Kill us slow, over time. Does not dishonor Balm to make law. They take our hunting grounds after."

"Then what kind of law would the Rauli tribe make if they won?"

"Same law, but drive away Balm tribe to die slow."

These guys really are two sides of the same coin. It'd be better if they could just get along already... Can't they just be a big gender-equal tribe? I'd been thinking a lot more about gender equality lately, especially with regards to family.

"So you only want Touya's child so you can use her to drive out the Balm tribe?"

"It is not only reason, but yes, for most part."

"...Very well, then. Let's strike up a deal. We can help the Rauli tribe win the current Pruning. We can help your tribe reach this... Treelord Tribe status. In exchange, give up on Touya entirely."

Wait, seriously?! You're gonna participate in the survival game?! I mean, I'd like to help Pam too, but... I can't give her a baby, that's way too much.

"...Can you win?"

"Hard to say, but it's better to take a chance instead of losing now and betting on the next decade, no?" Yumina replied with a little smile. The girl was emanating some kind of womanly intensity, I could feel it.

Come to think of it, after a decade or so my kid would only be nine or ten. They weren't thinking of putting her in a survival game then, were they?

"...If you say. If you can win, then Pam will be happy. But if lose like Pam expect, then Pam make a baby with Touya."

"I doubt it'll come down to that." Yumina and Pam gently smiled at one another. For some reason it was terrifying, though.

Apparently if Yumina and the girls temporarily joined the Rauli tribe, they'd be allowed to join the games. I couldn't help but find it a little weird, though.

It'd be like having eight foreigners come in and substitute for your baseball team. It wouldn't be the original team anymore, but just a group of some random guys.

"Yumina-dono, are you serious, are you?"

"I think this is the best compromise we can get. Are we all agreed?" I looked around, and found nobody disagreeing. Part of me did want to object, though. I didn't want to see the girls get injured.

But I knew that if I did object, they'd say something like... "You want to have a baby with Pam that much, huh? I see, I see... Is it because of her enormous boobs? Do you love boobs that much?!" I felt like some of them would worry, so I couldn't really speak my mind.

A lot of my fiancees had some insecurity about their breasts, which I thought was a tad silly. Most of them were still growing, so it was fine.

In terms of breast size, Yae was the biggest, then Hilde, then a considerable jump down to Linze, then Elze, then Lu, then Yumina, and... if you could call them breasts, Sue. Pam's knockers were bigger than Yae's though, so even she could get insecure.

Flora had mentioned some kind of dubious boob-enhancing medicine... but I wasn't so sure about it... If Yumina suddenly showed up with a back-breaking mega rack, I just didn't know how I'd feel.

"Then we will represent the Rauli tribe, we will. We will win the Pruning and gain the title for your tribe. But there is limited space for participation, there is."

"That's true… I guess if Pam goes in to rep her tribe, then the other four would be me, Hilde, Lu, and Yae, right?" Elze spoke up. This seemed fair, since Yumina and Linze weren't capable of close-range combat. The two of them were long-range fighters. Sue couldn't do much in the way of fighting, either.

Though she had been learning about wrestling from Lapis, Cecile, and Renne. She had a keen interest in those maids. I wondered if she wanted to become one or something.

At any rate, a plan of action had been decided upon. It was a little troublesome I couldn't get a word in edgewise the entire time, though.

"Ah, Yumina? I have a question…"

"Yes, Sue?" Sue tilted her head a little, speaking over to Yumina.

"Are we all going to go to the pruning?"

"I suppose so, yes. You can all cheer on the Rauli tribe as they fight. Plus, something may happen that leaves us needing a substitute."

"What about Touya?"

"He's central to this, so yes. I want him to cheer us all on as we fight… It'd also be nice to have him around in case of an incident."

I definitely didn't plan to just leave them to handle everything themselves. I'd accompany them as both moral support and actual support if anything bad happened. I had no idea what might happen, after all. I'd have liked to think there'd be no foul play, but there was no real frame of reference.

"Uhm… Touya's a man, though."

"Ah…" Everyone suddenly made the same noise. And she was right. If I called myself a guest with the Rauli tribe, my sex would be something people would find weird. If anything happened, I'd likely be told to butt out because I was an outsider, so I needed to make sure I was recognized as a tribe member. But I wasn't sure what to do.

"…Crossdressing, I suppose."

"No way! No way, damn it!" I finally mustered the strength to speak my objections to Linze's idle muttering.

The Pruning.

All the tribes in the Sea of Trees gathered beneath the Great Wishing Tree. It was said that they competed for the sake of honor beneath the judgment of their patron deity.

It was definitely something akin to a survival game.

We were participating as members of the Rauli tribe and aiming to win. That way we could secure the Treelord title for them. If we didn't, Pam would keep begging me for a baby… The Pruning would last a total of three days, so it wouldn't be awful in the end. Elze and Hilde were quite eager to fight. They were the kind of people who enjoyed testing their abilities. Plus, if things went well, we'd have solid ties with the tribe that controlled the Sea of Trees until the next Pruning.

Linze really wanted me to cross-dress, but I got out of it in the end. I was able to use [**Mirage**] to change my external appearance to that of a woman. Someone would find out if they touched me, but I was willing to chance it. I sent Pam back to the Rauli village using [**Gate**].

I also realized that holding conversations with them in their tongue would be difficult, so I learned the Null spell [**Translation**] for the occasion. It basically translated spoken words. To the listener, I'd be speaking their language. To me, they'd be speaking mine. Everyone won.

It was sort of similar to the innate communication that I had with Kohaku and my other summons.

For now... Pam, Yae, Elze, Hilde, and Lu were the ones picked to participate. I thought maybe we'd have to call on a substitute in case of injury, but apparently they had to lock in the teams they started with.

I wanted to participate, since it'd be pretty easy that way, but Pam and the other Rauli tribeswomen opposed the idea. Apparently if the Rauli tribe sent out a man, even a disguised one, to the Pruning, it would be considered dishonorable. Even if it was a case of me participating as an outside helper, they vetoed it.

It was a case of 'a man should be seen and not heard' with them. Honestly, it was a little scary being around them. Part of me pined for the safety of the Balm tribe.

After that, a month passed.

The day had finally arrived, and we headed to the Great Wishing Tree.

"Phew..." The tree was big. That was all I could really say about it.

What the hell... It's like several dozen meters across... Beautiful green leaves and branches spread out as far as the eye could see, all from a remarkably thick trunk. The tree wasn't nearly as tall as it was wide. It evoked the image of a fully unfolded umbrella with most of its grip cut off.

Sunlight broke through its leaves, illuminating the ground in dots and streaks. All the great tribes of the Sea of Trees gathered to bask in that light.

There were various tree stumps dotted around the Great Wishing Tree. Even the smallest were around twenty meters in diameter. Apparently they too were part of the big one, and used as staging grounds for duels.

There were two-hundred-and-forty tribes living in the Sea of Trees. But only one, the Jaja Tribe, hosted the Pruning ceremony. They were also known as the Judgment Tribe. Apparently they were the only tribe that the spirits had allowed to live at the base of the Great Wishing Tree. They had a fairly impressive claim to the land they called the Wishing Grounds. In exchange, they weren't allowed to participate in the Pruning. Apparently they worked like the priests of the region, conveying the will of the spirits to the other tribes.

"...There sure are a lot, huh..." I glanced around nervously. There were tribes of fat people, tribes of thin people. I saw tribes with weird head decorations, tribes with jangly bracelets... I even saw a tribe full of people with really bad mustaches, and a tribe of people clad head-to-toe in hooded green cloaks.

As I'd expected, most of the tribals here had a lot of skin exposure, both men and women. Nobody was sitting there with their junk hanging out, but some tribes wore so little that I didn't know what to look at.

"I am glad that we do not stand out, I am."

"Touya... It'd be best if you didn't gawp at women so much. You're disguised as one, after all." Lu made a backhanded little comment, so I replied with a cough as I stiffened my posture.

Everyone was wearing traditional Rauli clothing. In other words, chest wraps and loincloths. The girls were clearly embarrassed, so they wore little ponchos and wraparound skirts above the basic outfits. The clothes seemed suitable for Elze to fight freely in, though.

My [**Mirage**] projection was wearing the same as them, of course. But underneath it all, I was just wearing shorts and a t-shirt. I didn't want anyone to touch me and feel the sensation of clothing, after all.

Sue was also wearing the Rauli style, but she only looked cute. I didn't feel any kind of arousal when I saw her in it. The other girls, however... I had to avert my gaze, since they were pretty damn stimulating.

But hey, a lot of the tribes I was looking at were wearing even less, so this was modest by regional standards.

"Is there a reason we need to fight atop the stumps?"

"Yes, there is. The spirits offer their divine protection to the areas above the stumps. Fatal attacks are nullified within the confines. If someone tries to fatally strike someone in the head, for example, the person would merely be stunned instead. Lethal blows are simply downgraded." I didn't know how it worked, but spirits were certainly interesting. I wondered if it was similar to my [Shield] spell. Then again, it straight-up prevented fatal damage, so it was likely very different. It reminded me of mechanics in some games where the damage stopped at 1HP.

In other words, death wasn't likely during the challenge. Though, apparently people still died now and then. The stumps were around two meters off the ground, so if a participant fell off and hit themselves at an odd angle, the impact would kill them.

"What about magic?"

"Ah… It's all nullified. You shouldn't use fire-based techniques here, either. You'll be driven out of the region, and the Judgment Tribe will blacklist you." So even magic wasn't permitted. That meant Elze wouldn't be able to cast [Boost] at all. Everyone was equipped with regular weapons too, since enchanted ones became inert.

I could understand why they banned fire. If it actually caught and spread, it would've been awful. Apparently there was a large stream of water right outside the Wishing Grounds. Most people prepared food there to be safe.

There was seating arranged amidst the tree branches, so supporters could look down and cheer for their tribe. The trees were connected by suspension bridges.

"When does the first match start?"

"Soon. If we win against three other tribes, we'll be done for the day. That's how we advance to tomorrow's matches." *So two-hundred-*

and-forty tribes fight around three times... This round should bring them down to thirty. If today's matches are the preliminaries, then tomorrow's will be the finals.

A bell rang out from somewhere all of a sudden. All the chatter and murmur from nearby died down, and a voice called out to everyone.

"It is time. All but the participants must clear the area. All after this is the will of the spirits." A man from the Judgment Tribe, clad in a white uniform, spoke up. The spectators from the other tribes began to file off, moving toward the treehouse viewing platforms.

We decided to leave as well.

"Alright, guys. Make sure to do your best. Stay safe."

"I will do my best, I will."

"Gotcha."

"Leave it to us!"

"I'll try hard."

"Let's do it, then!" Yae, Elze, Hilde, and Lu followed after Pam to the tree stump where they'd do battle.

We moved up to the seats atop a nearby tree, climbing up some stairs and making our way to sit down. Our view of the fighting area was pretty damn good.

"I'm a little excited..." Sue leaned forward against the safety rail, staring down at the site below. Everyone in this particular tree belonged to the Rauli tribe.

There were around fifty spectators from this tribe in particular... I found it a little awkward, being the only man. Even though they physically saw me as a woman, they knew I was really a dude. I really should've thought about this harder. I could've just used [**Invisible**] or something.

Still, that would've made intervening harder in case of an emergency. It was better to be disguised as a member of the Rauli tribe, even if it was uncomfortable.

"Oh, Touya… Take a look over there."

"Hm?" I looked to where Linze was pointing, and saw rays of sunlight shining down like spotlights, focused on each tribe's representative. Slowly the rays moved, guiding each fighter to their stage.

I looked up toward the branches and saw them freely moving their leaves to guide the light. I couldn't believe what I was seeing. Did the Great Wishing Tree really have a will of its own? Apparently the lights decided who would fight who.

I didn't have too much time to think, because the battles began immediately. There wasn't even an opening ceremony.

"Are all the fights one-on-one?"

"Apparently if the first three win, then the remaining two don't have to battle." In other words, if one of the representatives was a great fighter, they could still lose if the other four were no good. If it was just a knockout tournament, one person could carry whole team, but that wasn't the case here.

A loss counted as either a surrender or one party being unable to fight anymore. Falling from the stump also counted as a loss. Cheating was forbidden, and any party found dishonoring his tribe would be disqualified.

I looked over at another stage and saw two people fighting. A large man brought down an axe onto his enemy's head. While it would've split open like a melon under regular circumstances, the guy just fell down where he stood.

It seemed like the spirits offered some kind of divine protection. Not all the wounds were prevented. Cuts and bruises still existed on the beaten man's body, so it was likely that all it did was prevent the killing blow. The man was simply unconscious instead of dead.

"Oh, the Rauli match is coming up." Yumina pointed at a place that was pretty far to see. I used [**Mirage**] and [**Long Sense**] in tandem to project a feed of the match into the air.

Amazed exclamations came from all sides of the crowd. It seemed my magic was still usable, since I wasn't the one on the stage.

I changed the size of the projection to a widescreen in front of the audience. Lu was the first one up to fight.

Her opponent was a tall guy wielding a lance. There was a height difference of about forty centimeters between him and her. Lu confronted him, wielding her dual daggers.

"Fight!" The white-clad referee brought down his hand, and Lu made a beeline for the man. He thrust his spear forward in response, but she repelled it using one of her blades and directed his attack elsewhere.

Lu did a sliding tackle, brought her left arm out, and pierced hard into the man's side.

A dull sound echoed as flesh tore. The spearman crumbled. She took him out in under a minute.

Roars of joy from the Rauli tribe echoed out.

Lu hadn't been training with me and Yae for show. From her perspective, the spear guy was way too dull in his motions.

Plus, twinblades like her were naturally quick on their feet. Their technique involved confusing and dazzling the opponent with fast footwork and distracting motions. They didn't have the raw strength of someone with an axe or broadsword, but they had boundless finesse.

That wasn't to say they couldn't defeat their foes in a single blow, either. Aiming for vital or weak spots meant very easy kills for them.

They specialized in agility and accuracy, so going for the kill was practically what they were made for.

Lu looked over to us and gave a triumphant wave.

Thus, the curtains fell on our first battle.

On the first day we won with relative ease, securing three victories and advancing to the next round. Nobody except for Lu, Elze, and Yae even had to fight their battles. It was decided in a mere three matches. We were on a hot streak.

Though, we were probably just lucky. Our opponents weren't particularly tough.

"Let's hope we can keep up this momentum tomorrow." I muttered quietly as I watched the sun set, the day leaving alongside it. We were in a forest by the river a bit away from the Wishing Grounds. The matches were all over, so everyone was preparing their meals.

Even the tribes that lost had come by to cook their meals. I figured they were going to watch the remaining matches regardless of their own losses.

We could've easily gone home and eaten in the castle, but the Rauli tribe had gone out in search of prey to cook up for us, so we decided to stay for some traditional tribal cuisine.

I took out a BBQ pit from [Storage], lit up the charcoal, and prepped it for cooking. Then, I pulled out salt, pepper, and some different sauces as well.

After a while, the Rauli tribeswomen came back with a bunch of what appeared to be various dead birds and rabbits. This place was a free hunting ground during the Pruning. For the rest of the ten-year period, only the Judgment Tribe were allowed to hunt here. There was more than enough wildlife to go around as a result. A vast number of animals were hunted and killed during the three days of the Pruning, but their numbers always replenished well enough before the next one came about. I wondered if this was another part of the spirit's blessing.

"Cooking outdoors surrounded by the beauty of nature isn't so bad now and then, is it?"

"Mm, you're right... Ah, Touya... This one's burning up!" Yumina was helping me grill dinner. We both looked like women from an outsider's perspective, so I hoped nobody thought anything weird of how close we were.

Eating meat alone wouldn't be much good, so I took out some peppers, onions, and pumpkins from [Storage] to use. I sliced them up, grilled them a bit, and put them on a skewer along with the meat. As a finishing touch, I slathered it all in BBQ sauce. A delicious combo, if I do say so myself.

"This is a first for me... but I quite like it." Lu smiled a bit as she cautiously bit into the food. I wasn't too surprised. A sheltered Princess of Regulus wouldn't have had this kind of food before. I was happy that she was happy.

Well, she might've been happy and relaxed, but I was more than a little uncomfortable being surrounded by so many girls. I was more than a bit out of my depth, for sure. I had a feeling that the former king of Lestia would be a little more proactive than me in a situation like this, though.

As I pondered to myself, I heard a noise behind me. Two beefy dudes were fighting against each other. They seemed to be in the middle of a dispute. It was kind of annoying, so I wished they'd go elsewhere.

"There's a lot of tribes here, so having them fight now and then isn't much of a surprise." Pam bit into the roast meat as she spoke. Apparently during the Pruning you weren't allowed to interfere during arguments, only the tribes of the people involved were allowed to speak up. The two quarreling men didn't seem to be active participants either way. Not that it mattered to me.

"Hm… Seems there are some strange people here. Oh wait, it's just the Rauli freaks." A few brawny guys came over, walking past the two arguing men. Their bodies were kind of like upside down triangles, as their chests were extraordinarily broad and muscular. They had scars and tattoos running along them as well. Their heads were shaved, except for the mohawks they had running along the middle. They definitely seemed like bad news.

"What do you want, Balm scum?" Pam chewed on her meat, a low glare directed toward the men. Evidently they were from the Balm tribe.

They sneered down at us with eyes filled with self-righteousness. Some of them were snickering and smirking at us, as well. I never wanted to be anything like these guys.

"We're pretty surprised you guys actually showed up this time. Weren't your best and brightest killed in that attack a while back? Pretty goddamn miserable, isn't it? But that's women for ya."

"You scum… Are you disrespecting our fallen?" Pam and the other Rauli tribeswomen lowered their stances a bit in order to make it easier for them to charge into battle. The Balm tribesmen switched their stances as well, as if anticipating an attack. A tense atmosphere quickly developed between the two sides.

"No, we're not disrespecting them… I just think that men from our tribe would've killed that monster in seconds flat."

"Pfft. You're ignorant and foolish, then. Even if the entire Balm tribe gathered together, they wouldn't do a thing to that crystal creature. It would've wiped out every last one of you."

"The hell'd you say?!" They were just yelling at each other now. Spitting venom without any clear aim. The whole situation reminded me of cats being at odds with dogs.

"Don't be an idiot! If the pathetic Rauli bitches could kill it, then we definitely could."

"Well, I'm sad to say that it wasn't our tribe that took it out. That honor goes to Touya here."

"Hm?!" *H-Hey now... Don't point!* The entire Balm posse turned their heads to look at me.

"This bitch?" A man from the Balm tribe came over toward me. He seemed to be around a hundred-and-ninety centimeters tall. He gazed down at me as if picking me apart. Then eventually, he smiled in a way that creeped me the hell out.

"You're quite a pretty little thing, aren't you? I'm a little smitten."

"Gross!"

"Excuse me?!" I couldn't help but say it. It wasn't exactly my fault! From my perspective, some big hunk of beefsteak was checking me out! It gave me the absolute creeps.

"You whore!" The enraged man tried to grab me by the arm.

"Don't you touch me!"

"Gaugh!" I kicked the man in the stomach, blasting him back a few meters. I couldn't afford to go easy on him. I was scared for my chastity!

"Bitch!"

"Get her!" I avoided all the Balm tribesmen who came after me, knocking them back one by one. I kicked them instead of using my hands. I didn't want to touch a single one of them. Honestly, I got a bit of a sense for how it must have been for some women in daily life... Being ogled by big creepy guys couldn't be a pleasurable experience for either gender.

"Get this bitch, get her!"

"Haaaaaaaaah!!!" A musclebound mass of man-meat was charging my way. It was horrifying!

"[Shield]!"

"Ghuawuh?!" I stopped them all in their tracks with an invisible barrier. They fell to the ground one by one. It was seriously sickening.

"The Balm tribe really is nothing to write home about, eh? All this struggling against one girl?"

"Guh..." Pam was laughing provocatively toward the fallen tribesmen. I really wished she wouldn't, though. I didn't feel like going for a second bout.

The remaining men had ashamed, red faces. From their perspective they'd been made a complete mockery of by a lone woman. There was no way a misogynistic tribe wouldn't be mad about that.

"Take your fallen and get outta here. It'd be a pain if you leave unpleasant clutter laying around." I was in complete agreement with Pam. If this persisted, I'd develop machophobia or something.

"Guh... We'll remember this!" The Balm tribesmen scurried off, dragging their defeated with them.

They were disgusting. Their eyes on me made me feel like a cheap piece of meat. I didn't ever want to be the kind of men they were.

"So that was the Balm tribe? They weren't all that tough."

"None of those were their tribe's champions. By Balm standards, those guys were meek. They were underage, too. Brats who haven't undergone the rites of passage." Pam answered Elze's query. I couldn't believe what I was hearing, though. From what I understood you were regarded as an adult in the Sea of Trees when you turned fifteen. That made those musclebound freaks even younger than me...! I thought they were creepy old guys.

There's just no way... There's no way they're the same age as middle-schoolers... Do they get some kind of intense training or something? Good grief... All of a sudden, I wasn't all that hungry anymore.

After the barbeque ended, it was time to rest. The tribeswomen were sleeping in shifts, some acting as alternating lookouts.

Ostensibly, it was to watch out for any monsters that lurked in the forest, but the threat of other tribes attacking was very real as well. Not every tribe was hostile, but we were certainly in the company of some violent types.

I was a little tempted to whip up a [Gate] and get the heck out, but leaving after hearing about the issue would've left a bad taste in my mouth.

I set up a barrier around us using [Shield] and decided to join the guard shift. The barrier was a temporary measure at best, after all. The five champions didn't have to take the night watch. They needed all their strength for the matches the following day. They were allowed to sleep all the way through the night. Having Sue join the watch would've been pointless as well, so we just let her sleep too.

It was just me and some Rauli tribeswomen. We were surrounding a blazing campfire, paying attention to the surroundings.

Linze and Yumina had taken the previous shift, so they were sleeping soundly in sleeping bags nearby.

Suddenly, I felt something strange. *What... This is...*

I stood up and walked deeper into the trees. The Rauli tribeswomen turned their eyes to me briefly, but then went back to what they were doing. They likely assumed I was taking a bathroom break or something.

Deeper and deeper I walked, and the presence I felt grew stronger as I walked on. It was one I recognized. One I had felt back in Ramissh.

I came to a clearing deep in the forest.

It was here. Right here. I'd found the spot.

"Can you hear me?" All the trees in the vicinity were suddenly jostled by wind. Moonlight shone down on me, illuminating the clearing.

Amidst the moonlight, a green glow began to reveal itself to me.

"Name thyself." The green light gradually changed its form. After a time, it took the shape of a young girl with dazzling emerald hair. She wore a one-piece dress, and her body emitted a faint green light. Her eyes shone like precious jade.

"You're… a spirit?"

"I am. I am the tree that presides over the Sea of Trees. I am the Wishing Tree incarnate."

"Just as I'd thought. I felt something similar to what I'd felt back in Ramissh. Though, the presence back then felt… dirtier. More toxic." I'd felt a faint presence from the Wishing Tree itself, but it was far more clear from this girl. If she hadn't fully manifested, I likely wouldn't have noticed her at all.

"You are the one…? You fought the Spirit of Darkness? Then you are the one who saved it?"

"Saved? I just ran in and exorcised it, really."

"Spirits are immortal beings, child. As the world turns, so too do we. The Spirit of Darkness will one day return to walk the earth.

More importantly than that... Just what are you? Why do you wear such a meager skin? What is that... smell? That feeling? Your body leaks power beyond even mine." *Hm... Can she sense divine power or something? I guess I was casting a lot of spells earlier... Maybe my power leaked out a bit when I was doing that.* I undid my [**Mirage**] and revealed my true form.

"I'm Mochizuki Touya. I'm the grand duke of Brunhild, a Duchy just to the north of this area. I'm currently subject to some... special circumstances, but for all intents and purposes, I'm a human."

"Just what is that supposed to mean...?" The tree spirit looked confused. I didn't really know what to do. It was clear my explanation of things wasn't too satisfying... but I had no idea if she'd believe me if I told her about God.

I didn't really feel like the situation was important enough to call God Almighty down here, either... But there was another option, even if she was a little awkward.

I opened up a [**Gate**] and plopped her in front of me. It seems she'd been sleeping in her bed when the portal opened.

"O-Owie! Wh-What's going on here, Touya?! That hurts, y'know?!" Karen, my dear sister, looked around with half-lidded eyes. She was wearing pink pajamas covered in pink hearts... It was a little weird.

I thought a bit about how I'd been treating Karen, and I realized I hadn't exactly been very gentle. But when I looked at her, I didn't really get the impression of a god. She was reckless, liked to play pranks, was terribly selfish, and stole my snacks!

Even so, I couldn't hate her. In a way, I really did feel like a member of her family. She also treated me like a little brother... so I was satisfied.

"Hey, Karen. Can you do that fwoosh thing that old man God does?"

"Huh? I don't know any fwoosh thing, y'know? Did you mean the Divine Release?"

"Yeah, that sounds about right." Light suddenly emanated from my sister's body, blinding everyone in the vicinity. It wasn't nearly as overpowering as God Almighty's, but it was definitely amazing. Even if she was a bit of a doofus, she was clearly a part of a divine pantheon.

"Hmmm... Are you perhaps thinking something impolite?"

"A-Ah, I'm sorry! F-Fowgihve me! L-Lemme goh!!!" She immediately began pinching my cheeks. It hurt like hell.

As I rubbed my poor face, the tree spirit had shifted herself to a fully prostrated bow.

It seemed that the divine aura was even effective against beings like her. Gods had incredible power, after all. Even if that god was... Karen.

"I can tell when you're thinking nasty things, y'know?"

"Agh, I'm sohrry! Fowgihve me!"

...Truly, the gods were terrifying.

"Then... Lord Touya is Lady Karen's..."

"Little brother in this world, yes. He's also an individual bestowed with power by the Almighty World God, y'know?"

That wasn't the full truth. It's not like I'd been bestowed power for any special reason, it was a simple case of chance. A mistake on the old man's part, really.

But still, the tree spirit seemed satisfied, so that was that.

"Why is a man like this present at the Pruning?"

"I'm here to cheer for my family members, some of them are participating. Ah, right... Don't rig the game in my favor or anything."

"I-I see..." Well, the Jaja Tribe was the group in charge of declaring the winner, so she probably didn't have anything to do with it.

Still, this situation was interesting. It seemed that, while Karen could suppress her divinity entirely... I wasn't capable of such a feat. That was how the tree spirit caught wind of me to begin with. It wasn't harmful for the time being, so I decided not to worry. It was probably a power I'd learn given time, anyway. Divine power wasn't something that could just be taught and passed on, it was an innate thing.

"So... this Pruning... is it a festival or something?"

"In the past, tribesmen would duel to settle their disputes. I used my spiritual protection to ensure they didn't lose their lives. Before long, it became somewhat of a tradition and a festival, though now it involves matters of honor and territory."

"Ah, that reminds me, y'know? I recall the Wishing Tree's spirit having the ability to nurture and protect life. Makes sense to me!"

That was interesting. The tree spirit had the ability to preserve life, that must have been one of her innate talents. But she didn't seem all that forgiving when you took into account those that died during the Pruning.

But still, if it could protect anyone anywhere, it's not like there'd be so much of a survival struggle in the Sea of Trees.

"This is quite interesting, y'know... Yes, I'd quite like to watch this Pruning first-hand. I'll cheer for Yae and the others!"

"Wait, you're not going home?!"

"You know... saying something like that after forcibly summoning a girl all the way here... It's more than a little rude... y'know?"

"Owowowowow!!!" I was mercilessly pinched once more.

The second day of the Pruning was upon us.

The tribes that had advanced to the second round were all ready to go. The day's agenda consisted of two matches. The eight winners would progress to the finals, which were to be held the next day.

In all honesty, I hadn't seen anyone who could match up to the Rauli team.

"By the way... which tribe won the last Pruning?"

"They called themselves the Panau tribe, but they're long-gone now." That wasn't terribly surprising. Ten years or so had passed since the last Pruning. It was a long time in a place built around survival of the fittest.

There were a lot of strong contenders, but they still didn't quite match up to our team. As far as our roster went, Lu was definitely the weakest link. Pam was stronger than her, and Elze was stronger than Pam when she employed [Boost] at least. Without any fortification spells, Yae and Hilde were as strong as Elze was with [Boost] too.

I couldn't imagine anyone beating our lineup, but we definitely had to consider weapon compatibility and the types of opponents they might face. It'd be bad if Pam, who wielded an Axe, was pitted against an agile knife-wielder. It'd also be bad if Elze, a close-range fighter, got paired up against someone with a spear. We also had to consider the fighting order as well.

Today's order was different to yesterday's. Yae was up first, then Pam, then Hilde, then Elze, and then Lu, the captain, was up last in the batting order.

"Wahoo! Yae's fight's about to begin, y'know?! Let's cheer! Knock it outta the park! Yae, Yae, she's our girl! If she can't do it, I'll totally hurl!"

"Karen… This isn't baseball… And it's not a cheerleading event, either." Karen stood by my side, prancing around like an idiot. Naturally, she was wearing the Rauli outfit as well. It would've been embarrassing if she had remained in her pajamas, but this was pretty embarrassing too.

Karen really stood out because she had a great figure. I shouldn't have been too surprised by her body. She was literally a goddess, after all.

As I was lost in thought, Yae easily struck her enemy down. The match-up was nothing to worry about. The enemy team looked completely dumbfounded. They must have sent a strong guy in, but if that was the best they had to offer, then we were gonna be just fine.

Our team won pretty handily. Both Pam and Hilde won their matches without a hitch.

"What's with this… Were they always this tough?" They'd been practicing every day, as well as completing the occasional guild quest. But still, even though they'd done daily training in our private facilities, the sheer speed of their increase in strength was something that startled me.

As I muttered and pondered, Karen turned toward me.

"Hm… I wonder… It might be that they're transforming into Wards, y'know?"

"Wards? What do you mean?"

"The divine power you hold is just the power of the gods… but it hasn't awoken completely in you. You can't use it on demand, y'know? If I was to describe what you were right now… I'd call you a demigod, y'know?"

Wait... I'm at that level already? I mean, I've felt my body shifting a bit, but still... That means I'm becoming less human even faster than I'd anticipated.

"Those I refer to as Wards are those that have received the blessings of a god. Touya, you're unconsciously distributing fragments of your divinity to the people you regard as family. You could consider it a blessing born from the love of a god... If we were to look at it on a more macro scale, we gods are all the Wards of World God. His almighty power is distributed to us, his family, y'know?"

Ah, I kinda get it... I think of those girls as my family, for sure. I want to see them protected. So that means I've made them into my Wards without knowing? Huh... So I guess Karen, and even me, are Wards of God Almighty.

"Those girls won't ever awaken to their own divine power or anything, but they may develop special abilities as a result of your presence. I'm certain that if things continue like this, they'll go down in history as some of the strongest humans."

"They'll get that powerful?!"

"God's love is no trifling matter, y'know? Beings that are loved by the divine simply become powerful. It's the natural order of things. The process will reverse if you ever come to hate them, though." *That's not gonna happen. I couldn't imagine hating any of the girls... But man, I didn't know I was making them more powerful by caring about them.*

"Still... you're only a demigod... They're a little powerful for... Oh... Oh!"

"Huh?"

"Oh, I see... That's how it is, then...? I suppose that's fine, y'know?"

"...Please stop reassuring yourself. Just tell me already." I grumbled over at Karen, who had suddenly begun muttering to herself for whatever reason.

"Ah, well... Those girls... are my Wards as well, it would seem."

"What?"

"I view you as my little brother, Touya. As family. Thus, they are my family as well, and I love them a lot. But my love for them isn't as strong as yours, y'know?" That made sense. She was the god of love, after all. I was a mere demigod. The girls had a good relationship with her, as well. It made me happy to see them getting along with their 'sister-in-law.'

"...Something wrong?" Linze called out to us, curiosity overtaking her. All the cheering in the vicinity made it impossible for her to actually hear our talking. Though, even if she had heard it, she'd have likely had trouble understanding.

"Nope, all good."

"I was just checking how much Touya wuvs you, Linze."

"I-Is that... so?! I-I, uhm... I-I also l-love you..."

"Ehehe! That's right, you do! You cutie pie!" Karen pulled Linze, who was now red as a beet, into a big hug.

Yep... That's a god's love, alright. I can see why they'd be her Wards too.

"Touya, take a look over there."

"Hm?" I looked over to the direction Yumina had pointed at, and saw two men standing atop one of the arena stumps. One of the men was large, flailing a great sword around. The other was bald-headed, more nimble, and wielding a bo staff.

The huge man was clearly from the Sea of Trees, but the other man seemed different. Looking at his skin color, he seemed to be of eastern descent. I wondered if he was a helper like we were.

He continued to deftly dodge each blow, wearing out the giant with ease. Eventually, he saw his chance and took it, driving the staff hard into his enemy's chest. The giant was felled in seconds flat, and the bald man was the victor. He bowed to his enemy and returned to the tribe he was representing.

He was strong, and clearly skilled, as well. He might've been hired by one of the tribes to win the tournament for them. By the way, completely unrelated, but try saying "balding bo brawler" really fast. Quite the tongue twister, right? I couldn't manage it more than three times.

I continued to look over, stupid thoughts like that in my head, until I saw another foreigner come out to represent that tribe. I was surprised to see a woman emerge, one who definitely looked out of place amongst the people here.

Her ears were pointed like knives, her pupils were a pure gold. There were traces of scales on her brown skin. On top of that, a broad tail jutted out from above her behind, and two curved horns grew out from her short black hair. I'd never seen anything quite like her before.

"She's from the Dragon Clan, isn't she?" Yumina whispered to me. The Dragon Clan… That was likely the case. The Dragon Clan was one of Mismede's seven demi-human clans.

"The Dragon Clan is few in number. Amongst the clans in Mismede, they have the least members, but they're a noble race of warriors, and they're said to be exceptionally powerful. It's my first time seeing one in the flesh." I hadn't seen any when we were in Mismede, either. Apparently the Dragon Clan didn't like to get involved in politics and generally only focused their interests on training and exercise. They didn't hold any high positions in Mismede, either.

She was wielding dark gray gauntlets. It looked like she was a brawler like Elze.

The moment her match started, she stepped forward in a flash. Within seconds, she was inches away from her axe-wielding foe. Her right palm shot out, almost imperceptible to the naked eye. A rumbling sound echoed out, and her opponent was rocketed out of bounds. She hadn't even placed her hand on him.

What the hell... Was that some kind of... release of stored energy? It couldn't have been magic, since that stuff's forbidden in the ring.

Just like the bald guy, she bowed and walked back to camp. She seemed pretty dignified. I wondered if they were students of a fighting school that taught respect to a defeated enemy, like in kendo or judo.

"Seems like winning won't be a complete cakewalk, then."

"Seems like it." We looked at the other battlegrounds and saw various tough-looking warriors. None of them seemed quite as imposing as the bald man and the dragongirl, though.

"Whuh?!" Karen suddenly made a weird noise as she looked down at a match. I wondered what it was she'd seen. I looked over and saw two people clashing swords. One was clearly a tribesman from the Sea of Trees. The other seemed to be an outsider from another nation. She was a swordswoman, wielding a blade in one hand and skillfully parrying her enemy's attacks. Her hair was short and purple, and her skin was a very pale white.

"Why... Oh... Oh dear..." *Incredible. She isn't moving at all... She's even blocking attacks coming from behind! How can she do all of that?! More importantly, how can she do all of that one-handed?!*

Eventually her opponent ran out of energy, and she put him down by striking him in the shoulder. With a single blow, he was down for the count. Her victory was sealed.

What the hell... She won without moving at all! That guy didn't seem like a pushover, either.

Sadly, the swordswoman's tribe couldn't match up to her, and her allies lost their following few matches.

"What... Why? Why is she here of all places?"

"Hm?" *Does Karen know her?* We saw her walking out of the Wishing Grounds, but she suddenly turned around. For whatever reason, she waved up at me and smiled.

What? Huh? Do I know her?

"Touya... I need you a moment. Yumina, I'll be borrowing your fiance for a moment, thank you."

"Hm? Alright, then." Karen dragged me away, way out of the Wishing Grounds, in fact. And, as if waiting for us, we came across the swordswoman. She was standing beneath the shadow of a tree, smiling.

"Yo."

"Don't 'Yo' me! What are you doing here?!" Karen folded her arms, an absolutely incredulous expression on her face. The swordswoman replied with a dry, fearless laugh.

"Officially, I'm here to aid you. Unofficially, I thought this might be fun."

"Hrmph..." The swordswoman's identity was completely unknown to me, but I had one terrible idea. I didn't want it to be true, though...

"Karen... This girl... Is she...?"

"Yes. One of my kind. The god of swords."

"The god of swords?!" I was right, and she was a combat god no less... A whimsical one who'd come down for fun, apparently. But still, it really felt to me like the gods had a little too much free time on their hands. Though, I suppose capturing servile gods was technically work, even if it felt more like a convenient excuse to goof off...

"A pleasure to meet you, I suppose. Though I've been spying on you now and then, so I feel like I already know you. Cool stuff, bro."

"Uh... Nice to meet you, then. I'm Mochizuki Touya."

"Oh, but uh... Hey, love god. What's the deal with that Karen stuff?"

"That's my identity down here! I'm his big sister, y'know? Mochizuki Karen! Has a nice ring to it, don'tcha think?" Karen puffed out her chest and cleared her throat. I had no idea why she was gloating. Then the swordswoman, or rather... the sword god, said something completely out of left field.

"Sounds cool, yeah. Alright, I'm a sister too."

"That's forbidden, y'know? I'm the only big sister around here!" Karen started blushing and laughing like an idiot. In response, the sword god clasped both her hands together.

"I'm telling you it's cool, man. I'm the second sister, so that makes me your younger sister. C'mon, Karen... Big sis..."

"I-I'm the older sister of two?"

"Yup, that's the one. I'm your little sis, yeah?" Karen made an exaggerated gesture as she tapped her chin. Eventually, she clicked her tongue as she looked between the two of us. It felt like some kind of stage play.

"Alrighty then! That's just fine, y'know?"

"Cool beans. That makes me your sister too, so be good to me." The sword god, who had inexplicably become my second sister, turned toward me and smiled.

And, just like that. I had another member of my family.

What the hell just happened?

"Touya has another sister?!"

"That's right, y'know? Her name is Mochizuki Moroha! Little Moroha! She's my little sister, y'know?"

"Nice to meetcha." The sword god... or rather, Moroha, my sister... shook Linze's hand. Everyone was baffled by the sudden appearance of my second sister. I couldn't blame them, since I was baffled too.

"So sorry we've taken this long to meet you. We're your brother's humble betrothed... It's an honor."

"Yup, good stuff. I know you. You're Yumina, that one's Linze, and that little one's Sue, yeah?"

"Ah, you know of us?"

"Yup. I've been watching you from up hi—"

"Letters! Letters! Yep! Karen's been writing letters to her, so that's how she knows!" My new sister was close to saying something stupid, so I quickly butted in. Moroha didn't seem the type to be able to read situations well. She seemed a bit airheaded. She was about as beautiful as Karen, but they were in two different categories. Karen was cutesy, but Moroha had an air of dignity and class about her.

She was really tall, and moved with a manner of grace. If I'd found out she was a member of a traveling dancing troupe, I wouldn't have been surprised.

"But still... what are you doing in such a place, hm?"

"Oh, uh... I tried to uh, force my way in and give it a go. It seemed pretty interesting, yeah? Ended up losing because my teammates weren't all that strong, though. But I basically came here to see about getting stronger." Moroha came up with a convenient excuse to deflect Sue's interrogation.

Apparently she was watching from above, but found the situation so interesting that she came down, forced her way into a tribe, and fought as a member like it was normal. The tribe treated her as if she was an old friend, though. I wondered if they'd been hypnotized... It shouldn't be impossible for a god to manipulate someone like that.

Strictly speaking, the two of them were forbidden from interfering with mortal affairs...

But apparently that just included them using their godly powers down here. If they did things in their extremely overpowered human bodies, then it was permitted. Their physical abilities were basically at the peak of mankind's potential. They weren't master-tier, but more monster-tier.

Still, even if I begged them to wipe out the Phrase or to restore Yulong, it wouldn't be possible. These useless gods were simply incapable of acting outside their respective domains.

"Getting stronger? Is it possible that Touya's skill with a blade is the result of your training?"

"Ah... Kinda, I guess. But Touya's swordsmanship is largely the result of his own techniques."

"But there's nobody in the world who can match Moroha, y'know? She's the greatest swordfighter on the planet." Karen started boasting, as if Moroha's skill was her own. That was just like her.

Well, she was a god too. I wondered if it might be possible to ask Moroha to train our knight order.

Still, she was the sword god… It was entirely possible she had no talent with axes or spears. Well, it was also possible she'd be okay with daggers and short blades, so I decided to ask her later.

"Oh, Yae's match is about to start! They'll advance to the finals if they win this." Sue's voice stopped my pondering as I turned to the stage. Today's matches would determine the top eight, and they'd go on to vie for the Treelord title a day later. But right now, sixteen remained.

"The Balm tribe have won and advanced, as well."

"As we'd thought, their champions aren't the guys who picked a fight with us earlier. They seem strong." That much was obvious. If they'd won with the cannon fodder I'd seen yesterday, they'd have been extremely lucky.

I decided to stop thinking about those weirdos and watch Yae's match.

Yae's foe was a tribal figure covered in tattoos. He held a tomahawk in each hand.

The moment the match started, he charged at Yae, raising his right hand high. Yae stepped back, avoiding him easily, then used her left hand to parry his right. She immediately jumped back, causing the two to be separated.

"It's Yae's win."

"Huh?" Moroha muttered to herself as she watched the match.

The man was closing in on Yae, but she simply continued to dodge his attacks, as if she was waiting for something to happen. And then, Yae moved. She deftly dodged his tomahawk and let her katana swipe out, cutting the thing in half. The weapon's blade fell out of bounds. Her swooping motion wasn't done. As her katana came back, it cut the other weapon to ribbons.

After that, her weapon came down upon the man's torso. He was defeated in a single blow.

"Yae's katana wouldn't be able to handle clashing with a destructive weapon like that. There'd be a chance that the blade would be damaged, after all. If she attacked him and he guarded with his weapons, it'd be the same story. She was biding her time until she could destroy the tomahawk. Even though she drew her blade and defeated him in one swipe, she could've ended it much sooner. The truth of the matter is that she was playing around. She was likely testing her capabilities, seeing if she could disarm him entirely. She needs more training, though."

Oho… I see… I don't fully get it, but she seems to… Moroha, the sword god, understood everything from a mere glance.

As for the rest of the match-up, Pam and Hilde won their rounds without any trouble, so the Rauli tribe would safely advance to the finals.

We'd succeeded in reaching the final bout with no complications.

"Hm?" As I looked over the other fights, I noticed the Balm tribe fighting a strange group.

They had elongated, skinny bodies with a hunched posture. The lot of them wore unusual masks on their faces, and claws on their fingers. Well… calling it a mask wasn't quite true, since it looked closer to a gas filter. For half a second, I could've easily mistaken them for a hazmat cleanup operation.

Their eyes looked… odd, as well. Almost like there was a kind of madness in them.

The Balm tribe's current fighter, a hefty man wielding a spear, wasn't doing too well. He had tons of tiny scratches all over his body.

He brought his weapon forward, but his aim was completely off. The man was breathing heavily and sweating up a storm, as well. He seemed beyond fatigued.

"Hm, poison?"

"What?" Moroha suddenly commented, much to my surprise. If it was poison... then their claws were probably laced with the stuff.

"It's not like it can kill or anything, but it seems like it causes dizziness, numbness, and drowsiness. It's not just on their weapons, but scattered across the entire stage."

"Isn't that against the rules?"

"You'd think that, but nope. Magic's forbidden, but nothing else. Sure, dishonorable stuff's forbidden too, but poison's a bit of a gray area. After all, some tribes use poison to hunt their prey."

I guess that's true. Feels kinda cowardly, though. I guess those skinny guys aren't exactly strong, so they use poison to make up for their lack of physical strength... It's a pretty clever way of compensating, I'll give them that.

I figured fighting with what you're specialized in wasn't something inherently wrong.

With the Balm warrior completely dazed, the hunched man charged forward and sank his claws into his enemy's stomach. Game, set, match.

After that round, the Balm tribe took a massive blow to morale. It didn't take long for them to lose the next two fights either. The poison-wielders, known as the Rivet Tribe, completely eliminated Balm from the proceedings without much fanfare.

"Huh, the Balm tribe lost."

"At least the Rauli tribe can rest a little easier now." This meant that the Balm tribe couldn't take the Treelord title and create a law that harmed the Rauli tribe, so that was a major relief.

Still, that poison was certainly worrying. If it was really scattered across the fighting stage, then they didn't even need to land a hit for it to be applied. They seemed to run defensive battles and wait for the poison to take effect. No point fighting when you can just wait your opponent out, after all.

Luckily the spirit's blessing prevented the poison from spilling out beyond the confines of the stump arena.

Though I suppose that was a subtle confirmation that the forest spirit and the judges approved of the poison. Speaking of which, the referee on stage was also affected by the poison, but it wasn't a lethal dose, so he'd be up on his feet within a couple of hours.

Regardless of it being a non-lethal amount, it was a major detriment. I decided it'd be wise for Yae and the others to prepare necessary countermeasures. They could find themselves facing that tribe, after all.

I had asked about the Rivet tribe's history in the Pruning, but apparently this was their first year. They were a relatively new tribe that had split off from a larger one. The original tribe used some poisons while hunting, but the splinter group was far more focused on it.

The tribes of the Sea of Trees weren't really families, but more like tiny societies. New tribes were born all the time, old tribes collapsed, or tribes merged with one another regularly.

"Oh." The brawler from the Dragon Clan was fighting elsewhere. She moved with the same deliberate gait, not expending any unnecessary movements. Just as before, her enemy was blasted away.

That was the tribe's third match, so the one she represented was also moving to the finals.

Each of the top eight tribes had some unique element to them. One of them wore full fur pelts of what looked to be jaguars, another used weaponry made out of animal bones, and so on. They had a lot of variety to them.

I was a little concerned about the challenge.

"Are we really doing this?"

"Yup. Don't hold back. Come at me any time. Magic isn't allowed, though." After I introduced Moroha to the other girls, Hilde and Yae requested that she spar with them.

Karen kept gloating about Moroha's swordplay, which sparked the interest of the two. But Hilde and Yae were still participating in the Pruning, so I couldn't afford to have either worn out. There was an important match coming up the following day. It would be too risky.

But even so, Hilde and Yae kept demanding that they see an example of Moroha's skills. So, after some arguing, it was decided that we'd hold a mock battle.

"Why do I have to do it?"

"There's nobody else for it, really." That was true enough. Even excluding Yae and Hilde, it wasn't like I could let Linze or Yumina go up against her.

It was just one of those things. Truth be told, I was a little curious myself. I gripped the mithril blade in my hands and faced Moroha down.

"Make sure to go all-out, yeah?"

"Then I'll start! Haaah!" I rushed in and swung my sword down, since I wanted to test something. My elder sister parried the blow with ease and spun around me, then swung her own sword at my back. I bent down and managed to dodge the blade, just barely.

I charged in again and tried a feint. I pretended to aim for her torso with a horizontal slice, but suddenly shifted my movement upward to go for her arm. However, before I could do anything, Moroha slammed right into me, knocking me off-balance. I fell on the ground and rolled a considerable distance away. She didn't chase after me, so obviously she wasn't even using her full power.

She smiled softly at me, but that only irritated me more. *Alright, she's not being serious, so let's go all-out!*

"...I give up." There I was, dazed and battered on the ground, in a state of utter surrender. It was impossible. Absolutely impossible. I managed to graze her one or two times, but I couldn't land a solid blow. If I had been able to use magic, it might've worked, but my swordplay alone was years behind hers. I couldn't hope to compare. She was the god of swords, after all. What was I expecting?

"Wowser, you were tougher than I thought. I even ended up getting a little serious. I bet if you keep it up and train a little harder you could reach my level, yeah?"

No thanks... Not interested in being your apprentice or anything. Besides, if I get that good with the sword, then I won't be able to fight fairly against anyone except you.

"I-I could barely even register their movements, I could not."

"S-Same here... Both of them... are amazing..." Hilde and Yae looked utterly flabbergasted, but they still managed to speak a little. Even if they thought it was amazing, there was a clear and marked difference between my skill and Moroha's. I didn't have the strength to say that to them, though.

"Hmm? Barely? That means you two could see our movements even a little though, yeah? Wow... you guys are pretty promising..."

Moroha smiled over at Yae and Hilde. The two of them looked at her with amazement. I could practically see the stars in their eyes. They seemed to be happy just being acknowledged by her, I figured.

"I intend to stay with Touya for a while, so I'd like to tutor you both in the ways of the sword."

"Really?! Th-Thank you, dear sister!"

"O-Oh goodness... You have my deepest thanks, you do." Both of the girls looked even more excited now. I couldn't help but feel it was the birth of two new acolytes of the sword god.

"Hmph... Seems little Moroha stole two of my sisters-in-law, y'know...?"

"I-I-I still respect you a lot, K-Karen..."

"Aww! Linzey-winzey! You're such a good girl, I love you!" Karen had Linze wrapped up in a bear hug for reasons completely unknown to me. Lu wasn't completely enamored like the other two, but she was a little interested in Moroha as well. She wasn't a complete sword nut like Yae and Hilde, so her reservation was understandable.

I finally regained the ability to move again, so I cast [**Refresh**] on myself and was fighting fit once more. *Geez... Looks like I've still got a bit to learn.*

I didn't know when exactly, but we'd attracted spectators. Our fight was pretty wild, so it wasn't all that surprising.

"Who are those people?"

"Guests of the Rauli tribe. Those ones aren't their champions, though."

"Goodness... but they're so strong. Why isn't that one participating for them?"

"I know, right?" The spectators continued their careless whispers around us. Why wasn't I fighting in the Pruning? That was obvious. I was a man!

I noticed the bald-headed staff wielder, and the Dragon Clan brawler amongst the crowd.

The bald man bowed his head in greeting as our gazes locked, but the dragongirl just gazed at me without moving at all. *Huh... Her right eye's golden, but her left is red... Does she have a Mystic Eye or something?* Her gaze was trained on me, but I suddenly felt a sense of incoming danger. I pulled out Brunhild and pulled the trigger within a matter of seconds.

A man suddenly fell out of a tree behind the dragongirl. I'd hit him with a paralyzing shot. He was still clutching a bow and arrow in his hands. Evidently, it had been trained on the dragongirl.

"Do you know this man?" I spoke to the dragongirl while pointing at the guy.

"...An earlier opponent, from a tribe I fought today." That made sense. It was a revenge attack. He couldn't handle losing, so he decided to hurt her. A man from the Jaja tribe came out and dragged the immobilized guy away.

The Pruning was fraught with danger, but it wasn't like attacking people in dishonorable ways wouldn't have consequences. In this case, his tribe would be banned from the next Pruning. Naturally, his people would turn against him because of the penalty he brought them. Exile would be a likely punishment in the end.

He would have to walk the Sea of Trees on his own for the rest of his life. That was punishment enough.

"I owe you a debt. My name is Sonia Parallem. I'm currently staying with the Ruluch tribe." The dragongirl, Sonia, slowly bowed her head to me.

"And I'm Rengetsu. Thank you so much for helping Sonia-san out of a potentially dangerous situation!" The shaved staff-wielder bowed his head to me as well. With a name like Rengetsu, I wondered if he was from Yulong or Eashen. I couldn't discern much about his ethnicity through hair color, either. He didn't have any, after all. Though, when I looked closely at his eyebrows, I did note that they were black.

"Rengetsu, where are you from?"

"...Hm? I'm from Eashen. Why?" *Thank goodness... Would've been a pain in the ass if this guy was Yulongese... Man, Eashenese people really like to travel a lot though; even Yae was wandering when I first met her. It's probably a case of training their bodies and learning the ways of the world.*

On the flipside, Yulongese people didn't travel much at all. Or rather, leaving the country was difficult to begin with due to the old government policies. There was a lot of red tape and difficult rules and regulations. It got to the point where people just didn't bother trying to leave. Their international news was also suppressed.

But the old regime had been completely destroyed, so refugees were spilling out of Yulong at an alarming rate. There weren't a lot of them, since most of the population had been annihilated by the Phrase, but I felt sorry for the nations that had to take them in.

"I'm Mochizuki Touya. I'm staying with the... Rauli... Tribe. Sorry, are you alright?" Sonia was glaring at me in a weird way, which kind of put a damper on my introduction. I wondered if she was invoking that Mystic Eye of hers.

"Uhm... what's up?"

"...I'm not sure if I wish to know the answer, but... why are you posing as a woman?"

Wait what? Did my [**Mirage**] *go on the fritz or something? Or can she just see through it.* I quietly asked Sonia, and she nodded.

"Ah, don't worry… I know some people have this kind of hobby, I'm not a judgmental person."

"W-W-Wait a second now! You're misunderstanding the entire situation here!" She thought I was some kind of cross-dresser or a man who liked to be seen as a woman. *It's just an illusion, I'm not even cross-dressing!* I took the two of them to a secluded area to explain myself.

The Rauli tribe wouldn't lose any honor because I wasn't one of their champions. Even if I was exposed, the only penalty would be me losing the ability to watch the matches. If that happened, I'd just cast [**Invisible**] and spectate that way.

"So… is your Mystic Eye the reason my illusion wasn't working?"

"Yes. I have the Mystic Eye of Revelation. I can negate visual trickery. Any kind of visual effects caused by magic are completely undone by my right eye." *Incredible. So she can probably negate blinding spells as well. Oh, but then again… if she's caught off guard she might not be able to trigger it in time.*

"This isn't a huge deal, but I'd prefer it if you both kept quiet about it."

"Alright. That makes us even, then. My debt repaid to you for saving me."

Good to see some reasonable people around. These two are actually pretty nice, easy to talk to… According to the duo, they were adventurers who traveled the world together in order to improve. Apparently they were just in the region, and two champions of the Ruluch tribe had come down with sickness, so they took their place.

"We were lucky enough to see your battle earlier, Touya. You're certainly something, but… The woman you fought, who is she?"

"Aha. That's one of my big sisters, Moroha… She's the middle child, and I'm the youngest. Winning against her is pretty much impossible. When it comes to swordplay, she's peerless."

"Peerless, you say…" The look on their faces spoke plainly. They didn't believe me. Didn't change the truth, though.

For the time being we decided that we'd cheer one another on. After that, I parted with them.

"So, you were here?"

"Hm? Pam?" After I split from the two of them, Pam showed up. Her figure revealed itself from the shadows, faintly illuminated by the moonlight.

"The Balm tribe isn't gonna win, you can rest easy."

"That's true… but I'd still like to see about… planning for the next Pruning. I'd really like your child after all, Touya."

"You said you'd give up on that if we won."

"I know I did. And a Rauli woman doesn't break her promises." Pam sulked a little bit. Clearly she was disappointed.

"If we win, will you be using your law to banish the Balm tribe?"

"Mm, that might work out… But we've come this far, so I was considering some other laws. It's hard to think about what might benefit the Rauli tribe, though…" Pam pondered quietly to herself.

Something to benefit the Rauli tribe, huh…? I guess the natural one would be a law that benefits women. The Rauli tribe is opposed to gender equality, after all… Still, it'd be best if they didn't mix their gender politics into the laws of a whole region.

The disparity between men and women was only present in the Balm and Rauli tribes, after all.

Though, if I had to admit it, I would say that women probably had it rougher than men across the board in the Sea of Trees.

"Oh! How about making it so only women can participate in the Pruning?"

"Don't be an idiot. That'd definitely make people freak out."

Guess you have a point. The other tribes would hate it. There are some tribes with mighty women, but most of the warriors are men.

"Then what about making two separate Pruning ceremonies divided by gender?"

"Hm… That… could be interesting… If it was split by gender, my tribe would have an incredible advantage." Pam began to think once more.

Hey now, I wasn't being all that serious… But I guess having men and women fight each other in the same contest is a little unfair. The Olympics has two separate categories, after all. The body of a man and the body of a woman are fundamentally built for different things. That's a biological fact. It's not discrimination, but simple differentiation.

"But if that rule's established, tribes will likely participate in both divisions. Won't that put the Rauli tribe at a disadvantage? The Balm tribe, too."

"That's fine. Actually, I'd prefer it. If we put this into effect, the tribes in general will start to value women more." Well, that made sense. I didn't think about it from that angle. If women were put into an enforced category, then they'd become more active in society as well.

Although, if the women of all the tribes started to find their strength and independence, they may look for a place where that strength is better respected. They might even end up finding themselves involved with the Rauli tribe before long. That'd result in the tribe becoming stronger… Pretty cunning, really.

Improving a woman's place in society was definitely not a bad thing... At least it shouldn't have been, but the manly man in me felt a little mixed. I might've proposed something strange.

The tree spirit would have to grant two laws if the Pruning was split into two, though... That'd probably be fine.

It's not like the spirit actually granted the law, they just determined whether it was appropriate or not. Enforcing it was down to the tribes themselves.

"I'll consult the rest of the tribeswomen. This could change the Pruning for the better." Pam ran off with a spring in her step. As I wondered whether I'd done the right thing, the tree spirit suddenly appeared next to me. She was glowing as usual.

"That was not a bad suggestion. Women may end up being treated better in the Sea of Trees as a result. While the Rauli tribe is an extreme example, the other tribes have women with potential as well..."

Hm... I see, I see... Then it might not be so clear-cut... The Rauli tribe might even make themselves some rivals with this law.

I decided to head back to everyone else. The tree spirit vanished as well, just like that.

She didn't ask about Moroha, which made me wonder if the sword god had concealed her divinity entirely. It was still leaking from me, though... I had no idea how to turn off the faucet, so I had a feeling it'd cause me trouble again before long.

On my way back, I suddenly turned around. I saw shadowed individuals heading deeper into the forest. *Are those... members of the Rivet tribe? Yeah, those masks are too unique to be anything else.*

At the time I just assumed they were going off to the bathroom or something. I didn't think anything of it. Sadly, that proved to be a terrible mistake.

The third day of the Pruning had begun.

The day had come to end this conflict. The remaining eight teams would fight, and the Tribe of the Treelord would be determined by sundown.

Pam spoke about my proposal to her fellow tribeswomen, and it was met with an enthusiastic reception. I was a little worried that maybe I'd done something unnecessary, but I decided to just forget about it. Whatever would come to pass would come to pass.

The first four matches would be held at the same time. That way, the top four tribes would be decided quickly. After that, two matches would be held one after the other to determine the finalists. Then, the finals would begin.

The tribes all faced each other, atop the tree stumps in the Wishing Grounds.

I wasn't actually sure why the arenas were in the shape of stumps… Apparently they vanished into the ground once the Pruning was over. I figured it was more of the spirit's power, or something. I decided it wasn't worth thinking or worrying about.

"Our first matchup is… with a tribe of strange ones." They were draped head to toe in birth feathers, wore mantles around their necks that made me think of bird wings, and had head ornaments fashioned from the skull of what I could only assume to be giant birds. *That's… certainly an ensemble… I wonder if they're a science ninja team or something…*

Once the match began, the bird guy jolted forward with incredible speed. *Whoa! That guy's fast!* Elze, who was watching him, didn't move a muscle.

The man kept running around Elze, charging in for feints and real attacks at his own discretion. He kept trying to fake her out, charging in only to pull back, and jumping or rolling around like a madman. Even so, Elze didn't move.

Suddenly, he boosted his speed even more, using the momentum to get behind Elze's back. Then, he pulled out a dagger and aimed right for her neck, but she sidestepped it masterfully. In a flash, Elze delivered a catastrophic chop that smashed the bird skull the man was wearing. I was fairly sure it would've smashed his actual skull if the protection wasn't in place. *Ouch.*

The bird tribesman had fallen and he couldn't get up. He wouldn't die, but it really felt like a serious case of overkill.

After Elze, Yae and Hilde both achieved easy victories. The Rauli tribe was the first to advance to the semi-finals.

"Incredible, y'know? They just totally overwhelmed them!"

"If they were going up against slow and brawny opponents, their tactics would have worked. Using speedy disruptions is smart, but they were no match for Elze and the others. No match at all." Like Karen and Moroha said, it was a case of a bad match-up for our enemies. The girls had become even stronger since the first day, somehow. It was terrifying…

…Wait, don't tell me that they've become Moroha's Wards too?! Yae and Hilde have been hanging out with her lately, but… Oh geez… That's totally what happened, huh?

Well, it's not like that's a bad thing. I just feel a little bad since they're all caught up in my weird circumstances now.

"Ah, Touya. Look over there."

"Hm?" Linze pointed over at Rengetsu, the guy with the bo staff. He had just felled his own opponent. The Ruluch tribe had achieved a consecutive victory as well.

Thus, the top four tribes had been determined. One of them was the poison-wielding Rivet tribe, as well.

I'd prepared filtration masks for Yae and the others as a last-ditch countermeasure, just in case we were paired up with them.

The final four were:

The Femme Fatales, the Rauli tribe.

The Poisonous Pests, the Rivet tribe.

The Martial Masters, the Ruluch tribe.

And the Remna tribe, who were really strong or whatever.

With that, we had four basic Japanese starting syllables. Ra, Ri, Ru, Re! Ro was missing, though... Didn't get a full set.

"Should we be worried about the Rivet tribe?"

"Well, there's also the Ruluch tribe, since that's the one with Sonia. Depending on who you're up against, that could be close." It'd be pretty easy if they were against the Remna tribe. All they had going for them was physical ability. Though it would've been bad if they got caught by one of them. The men from Remna had the physical strength to shatter a bear's spine with one arm. The girls just had to keep out of their reach, which wouldn't be too hard due to how simplistic their style was.

"Oh, the first match is starting. Oh my..." Sue gestured to the stage. The branches began to rustle and creak as sunlight shone down onto the two selected teams. Rauli and Ruluch.

"It's Sonia's group... This'll be a tough one." In all honesty, I didn't think Lu had a chance if she went up against either of the those two. The same probably applied to Pam. I wondered if Yae and Hilde would be able to match up to Sonia. Elze would likely lose against Rengetsu due to it being a bad match-up. If Pam and Elze were knocked out by Rengetsu and Sonia, and Lu lost her fight... We'd be done for.

I still thought we had a higher chance of winning than losing, though.

Both sides moved to their respective positions on the stump arena. You could see clearly from up here, but the participants didn't know who they'd be fighting until just before the battle began.

"Oh dear..." Lu was matched with Rengetsu, and Elze was matched with Sonia. That was a bit worrying. Still, even if they lost, Yae, Hilde, and Pam could pull out a win. I was only really worried about Pam.

It would basically be a certain victory for us if Lu or Elze won their battles.

Elze had the best chances of winning, but it was basically a duel between brawlers. I wasn't certain of her chances with Sonia. If she was able to use [Boost] she'd have the upper hand, but such a luxury was not afforded.

The first match began, so Lu and Rengetsu walked toward the middle of the stump. There was a serious height disparity between them. Rengetsu was over a hundred-and-eighty centimeters tall, while Lu wasn't even at a hundred-and-forty-five. It looked like an adult prepping to fight a child. I wondered if people would consider it dishonorable if Rengetsu beat her.

The referee called the start of the fight. Lu took an offensive stance with her twinblades, and Rengetsu prepared his staff. The man's staff was a gleaming silver, and had each end tipped with gold. At a glance I'd guess it was a mithril and orichalcum weapon. He handled it like a pro. His strength was clearly nothing to sniff at, but if the staff was actually made of iron and gold instead of light metals, I'd have been even more terrified.

Lu dashed forward, and Rengetsu responded by moving his staff. She scraped down the side of his staff with one of the blades and tried using her forward momentum to jump at his chest. Rengetsu responded in kind by thrusting the bo staff into the ground and pole vaulting over her. His agility was nuts.

Hmph... I guess this guy really is one level above. He saw through her entirely.

"Lu... Will Lu be okay?"

"Come now, she won't let it end so easily." Lu held her swords, spun them around, and charged right back into the fray. She sent blow after blow against him, attempting to wear him down with an overwhelming barrage. She was both light on her feet and monstrously relentless. It was almost scary... However, I noticed something off about her movements.

"Wow... She's moving just like a brawler, yeah? Did Elze teach her that?" Moroha understood immediately. She saw exactly what was going on. Lu's movements were nigh identical to Elze's deft footwork. It seemed that she'd been learning well.

"Guh!" Rengetsu endured the assault using his staff, refusing her access to his vital spots. Still, Lu had the upper hand, since she was wearing him down. After a while he found himself cornered, sweeping his staff to the side and taking a few steps back.

Lu, however, relentlessly pursued him. That was when Rengetsu changed his attack plan. He suddenly dashed forward, tossing the staff at Lu's feet. She stumbled, and he drove his hand against her breast as she lost her balance.

"Augh!" Lu fell to the ground and rolled off to the side before getting back up. That definitely hurt.

Rengetsu, you bastard! What do you think you're doing to my princess, huh?! You bald bastard! I'll kill you! My thoughts briefly grew incomprehensibly angry.

...Calm down, calm down. This is just a match. Let it go, let it go. You'll get revenge later... You'll [**Slip**] *the bastard good.*

This time it was Rengetsu's turn to unleash a barrage of attacks on Lu. She could barely avoid the staff as it jabbed against her, but then she dropped the sword in her left hand and caught the pole beneath her armpit. Still, just as she was about to launch her counter, Rengetsu let go of his staff.

"What? Uwah!"

"Haaah!!" Lu suddenly lost her balance entirely. Discarding his staff, Rengetsu held out his palm and yelled loudly. In an instant, an invisible force seemed to shoot out and knock Lu backward.

Wait, is that the same explosion of force I saw Sonia use? I guess they're allies, so it's not too surprising.

Lu managed to maintain her composure and, after flying through the air, gracefully landed on her feet. Out of bounds, though.

"The winner is Rengetsu!" The referee announced the winner just like that. A thunder of clapping and cheering echoed out from across the venue.

Lu was defeated. She was simply knocked away at a bad angle. If she was only a meter closer to the center, she'd have been okay.

"So... she lost."

"Hey now, we weren't going in expecting smooth sailing. Even Lu knew she might lose." I patted the sulky Sue on the head, then gazed down at Lu. She collected up her weapons and shook Rengetsu's hand. She seemed really disappointed. There was no doubt she wished she could've carried on. But to me, she'd done incredibly.

"Well, now that this has happened, we really need to win the next..." Elze and Sonia both made their way to the stage.

Both were melee brawlers, and they both signaled their readiness by smacking their gauntlets together.

They took their stances opposite one another, looking at the other dead-on. The referee raised his hand and looked between the two. Then, he brought it down in a flash.

"Begin!"

Whoooooosh. They both charged toward one another at full speed. Their fists were flying toward their enemy's face, and both hits connected. It was an incredible cross-counter, on both sides. *Whaaat!!! That's way too fast! And why are they smiling?!*

"You're... pretty good."

"Y-You too."

Oh come the hell on, what are you guys?! Gang leaders brawling on a riverbank?! They separated and immediately began exchanging blows. Elze unleashed a straight right, and Sonia absorbed it with her gauntlet. Sonia then made for a left hook, but Elze parried that as well.

The sound of metal was intense.

Clang. Thwack. Thump. Thud. Scrape! The sound of metal on metal permeated the air around the stage. It was terrifying. The terror was amplified by the fact that both of them were laughing. They were smacking the hell out of each other, and cackling. It was seriously scary! I doubt anyone would understand how freaked out I was!

Alright, that's all folks! Come on now! Bye bye, okay! That's it!

I was uncomfortable, like a man possessed.

Metal continued to clash, over and over again. Relentless. Strike, block. Strike, block. Strike, block...

It looked like they were following some unspoken rule of taking turns to hit one another. The speed slowly ramped up until it was basically just two flurries of blows storming on at each other.

"Hiyaaaaaah!!!"

"Gaaaaaaaaah!!!" The sound of scraping metal rang out as their fists connected again, both of them going in for a straight right.

For a moment, the two of them stood still, grinning and laughing all the while. I had no idea what high they were riding, but it was frightening.

Then, both of them jumped back at the same time before rushing in and launching a flurry of kicks. The greaves on their legs clunked and chimed as they smacked against each other. After that, the metal sounds of clashing gauntlets repeated itself once more.

"Hiyaaah!" Elze performed a spin kick. Sonia tried to block it, but the momentum was too strong, resulting in the girl being pushed further back. Elze charged forward, intent on following it up, but Sonia quickly dodged to the side and lashed out using her tail.

Elze took the full brunt of the tail whip and was knocked back a bit herself.

Sonia went on the offensive now, attempting to land a drop kick, but Elze brought both arms up in a cross and blocked it perfectly. Sonia kicked against Elze's gauntlets and used the momentum to create some distance between the two.

The heated battle continued to rise in temperature, with the offensive and defensive flickering making the crowd get excited.

"Moroha, what do you think's gonna happen, y'know?"

"Hard to say. This isn't a battle of blades. Unfortunately, my knowledge when it comes to fists is a little more lacking. Elze has the superior mobility, yeah? But Sonia's definitely kicking it big with the power. The gap between the two isn't all that huge, though. Sonia also has an ace up her sleeve, one she's yet to play."

You mean that energy release thing... Elze hasn't really given her a chance to use it so far, since there haven't been any openings at all.

Elze was unable to use her [**Boost**] too. Yae had watched several martial arts videos on my smartphone, but so had Elze. She learned a lot from researching how many different people fight.

The two were slowly becoming a little slower in their motions, likely because they were running out of energy. Regardless, their fists kept flying back and forth, over and over again.

Elze made a mighty sweep toward Sonia, but she managed to avoid being knocked off-balance by stabilizing her tail's position. That tail of hers was really something. I wondered if it kept her more stable and balanced than regular humans.

Sonia then used her tail to attack Elze. Elze steeled herself and took the brunt of the attack with her gauntlets. Then, she gripped the tail firmly, pulled on it, and tossed Sonia over her shoulder with all the strength she could muster.

"Haaaaaah!!!"

"Guh!" Sonia had been knocked prone, and Elze jumped in to land the finishing blow. But alas, Sonia rolled to the side and deftly dodged the attack. She rose to her feet, braced her body, and held out her palm. *Shit, not good!*

"Haaa!!!" With a loud boom, Elze was knocked flying. She rolled all the way across the stage and just managed to stop herself from falling out of bounds.

Goddamn! That was dangerously close to being the same as the Lu situation.

I knew that stance meant bad news. It was definitely some kind of invisible ranged attack. Elze didn't even get hit by it directly, but she was still knocked a fair bit away.

Elze was on her knees, and looked to be in considerable pain. Sonia, refusing to let up, began charging toward her once more. Elze stood up and blocked it, but the pain from the previous attack was still taking its toll. Elze was shifted to the defensive position, and the stage's boundary line was right behind her.

"Haaaaaa!" Sonia brought her right fist rocketing forward, but Elze caught it using her left. Sonia then followed up with an attack from her left hand, but Elze caught it using her right! Sonia raised her leg in an attempt to kick Elze, and that was when Elze used her grip on the girl's hands to start throwing her backward.

Elze brought her own leg up, placing the flat of her foot on Sonia's abs, and then began to hurl the girl upward with all of her strength.

It looked pretty unconventional, but it was some kind of overhead throw. Elze's head was leaning over the edge of the stage as she was on her back and hoisted Sonia into the air, though the rules stated your whole body needed to be out for it to count as a loss.

"Ghhh...!" It looked like Elze was about to succeed in throwing Sonia out of bounds, but... Sonia twisted her body around and lashed out with her tail, escaping from Elze's grip. Her body leaned backward, toward center stage.

Sonia was barely balanced on the edge of the arena, but she wasn't out of bounds. Suddenly, Elze came up to her from the front.

"Hiyaaah!" Elze screamed and brought a right straight headed directly for her enemy. And, by reflex, Sonia brought her arms up to defend against the hit. Avoiding or dodging wasn't feasible given her precarious situation.

Unfortunately for Sonia, the punch was just enough to ruin her balance, sending her hurtling into the air and out of bounds completely. Game, set, match.

"The winner is Elze Silhoueska!" The referee declared the winner, and the audience went wild. The two were applauded and cheered for.

"She won! Elze won!" Sue cheered merrily. But honestly, it felt like more of a draw. Elze was really hurt. Neither had managed to knock out the other, either. But still, I believed that if it was a real fight, one unrestrained by rules, Elze would've come out on top.

Elze shook Sonia's hand as we all clapped for her.

We had one loss and one win. So long as two more of our remaining fighters won, we'd be in the finals.

I thought Pam might be a dead weight, but it was wrong of me to feel that way. She performed like a champ in the third match and won in under three minutes. She knocked her foe out of bounds with unrelenting fury. The girl was like a whirlwind.

Yae was up after that, and came out on top with the greatest of ease. With that, the Rauli tribe easily secured its success over the Ruluch tribe. We'd made it to the finals.

"Somehow, we managed." I felt nothing but relief. The Ruluch tribe was the tribe that I had the most concerns about, so the final match was probably going to be a cakewalk.

I cast [Refresh] and some recovery magic on the participants. Just to be safe, I prioritized Elze and Lu, though. They needed it the most.

After that I cast [Slip] and made Rengetsu fall over repeatedly. He was sitting with the rest of the tribesmen that he'd represented, when suddenly he slipped and bashed his head on the ground. He stood up, utterly confused, and had no idea what was going on. He was on soil, so he wasn't hurt or anything, just shocked.

"What are you doing...?"

"Well... he hurt Lu, so I kinda got mad."

"That dragongirl hurt me, too!"

"Well, I know... but I couldn't really get angry at your fight. It was like watching a hot-blooded drama." Elze grumbled slightly and pouted. Well, it wasn't my place to intrude on the fast-paced battle between two girls. Still, if her opponent was a guy, then I'd have definitely tormented him or something...

"Either way, we're in the finals. One more to victory. Ah, take these." I handed a small vial of pills that kind of looked like the round thing in ramune soda to Elze and the others. It was an antidote I had Flora produce. It completely eliminated poison from the human body.

"There'll be poison scattered on the stage, so wear your masks before your turn comes. Then when it's time for you to actually fight, remove your mask and eat one of these the moment your round begins. That way their claws won't do anything to you, since the poison will be nullified. You don't need to worry about the passive poison, either. One pill should last about ten minutes, so try to win before then. Take three of them." After that, the girls returned to the Wishing Grounds. If poison was one viable method, an antidote was another. It wasn't magic, so it didn't go against the rules.

We returned to our seats in the audience, but quickly found some commotion going on.

Once we took our seats, we discovered that the Rivet tribe had already won their battles and been declared as the finalists. No matter how you looked at it, that was a little fast.

"The Remna tribe moved to attack when the round started, but they collapsed immediately. It seems the Rivet tribe has a blowgun. Their dart was extremely narrow too, so nobody could see it… Even though they used masks to defend against the scattered poison, they couldn't do a thing against poison directly entering their bodies! Plus, the poison acts incredibly quickly. It's not immediately lethal, but if the affected doesn't get medical attention fast… Well, it could be ugly." I looked down on the grounds as Moroha spoke to me, and I saw Elze handing over antidote pills to the fallen tribesmen. *Yup, good work… I gave them all a few, so sharing is caring.*

"Still, you said a blowgun? It's pretty impractical unless the poison alongside it works." If they'd been using throwing weapons like shuriken or knives, that'd be another story… Still, this poison was something to consider. It was definitely some kind of effective toxin, but it didn't actually kill or anything. I wondered just what the poison was.

If it had paralytic effects it could be a neurotoxin, like the tetrodotoxin from a pufferfish. However, that toxin definitely didn't take effect immediately. Tetrodotoxin was one that made you numb over a long period of time, then killed you.

I hadn't seen any pufferfish in this world, either, so it was hard for me to tell. A more likely answer was just that I wasn't familiar with the poisons of this world. Flora really was incredible, since she'd practically made a cure-all panacea for poison.

That being said, I was sure I could remove the effects with [Recovery] as well. Better to be safe than sorry, though.

The final stage in the Wishing Grounds rose up.

This one was a bit bigger than the stages used for matches up until now. All five champions from either tribe stood on either side.

Chapter III: The Pruning

Yae and the girls were wearing the filtration masks like I'd told them to, and so was the referee. It was kind of funny, seeing everyone in those things.

The finale had begun.

Yae was up first. Her opponent was the lanky, hunched man that I'd seen earlier. The one with the claws. There was a little opening on the front of his mask, where something similar to a tube jutted from. That was likely where the blowgun poked out.

He wore the mask to avoid being poisoned, which must have meant that the blowgun wasn't attached to his mouth. I wasn't entirely sure how he got the air through it to shoot out the dart. His mask must have been designed in an interesting way.

Yae tore her mask off and swallowed the pill. That would render her completely immune to their toxic trickery. Her masked foe looked at her in a somewhat confused manner, but he readied his claws all the same. In response, Yae drew her katana.

"Fight!" Yae thrust toward her foe in a blazing display of speed as soon as the match begun. The man panicked and attempted to fire the dart from his blowgun. Yae raised a hand to protect her eyes, staying completely on target. The dart pierced her hand, but she ignored it and instead tackled her enemy and landed a single blow in the middle of his stomach.

"Ugahagh!!!" The man coughed and sputtered unintelligibly as he blasted his way out of bounds.

"The winner is Kokonoe Yae!" It was over in a flash. The entire place fell silent for a moment, nobody knowing what to say. But then a roaring cheer engulfed the crowd like a wave.

She must have known the blowgun was coming. Presumably she'd heard about it from one of the Remna fighters.

"Our poison didn't work...? No way!" Hilde's enemy, a younger man who looked kind of like a frog, muttered in frustration. He mustn't have been able to believe what he had just seen during Yae's round, but it was too late for him as well. The guy looked like he was shaking a bit, too.

Just as Yae had done before her, Hilde charged forward recklessly, completely tanking the poison dart and sending the froggy fellow to his defeat.

"Gurribitaaagh!" The poison was inert, which completely crushed the enemy morale. Pam prepared her axe as her enemy, a large trembling man, stood before her.

He was no match for her. His dart did nothing either, and Pam was completely victorious. Her axe came down mercilessly on his head.

"...Gh!!!" The last of Rivet's champions fell unconscious.

"The winner is Pam! Thus, the Rauli tribe takes the title! They are the new Tribe of the Treelord!" It was a consecutive three-person finish. A little boring for a finale, honestly. But even so, everyone in attendance cheered and applauded like their lives were on the line. The Pruning had finally concluded.

Pam put on her war face and cried out to the heavens. In response, the entire Rauli tribe gave their best unified war cry.

That was that. *All's well that ends well.*

...Or so I thought, but then I felt it.

"Huh...?" The ground was rumbling... Shaking, even. I suddenly saw every tree outside the Wishing Grounds begin to wither and dry up. Their leaves all scattered to the ground.

What the hell?!

"Guhahah... We'll be taking it now... The spirit's power, I mean...!" One of the fallen members of the Rivet tribe muttered that.

The ground began to rock and quake. Shockwaves began rippling everywhere as more trees died and more leaves fell to the ground.

"Wh-What is that?!" I heard someone screaming out, and I turned to look. I saw... trees. Enormous trees, moving. *Walking* in our direction. As it turned out, whatever was happening hadn't even begun yet.

"Wood Golems... But they're way too big! Did they end up becoming Behemoths or something? But why are there so many...?!" Several wooden Golems covered in bark were stomping this way, destroying anything beneath their feet. They were each over twenty meters tall. Shape-wise, they were the same as a Mithril Golem, size-wise they were not.

One... Two... Three... Yup, there's at least ten. Did they sap the life out of the local plant life or something? The closest Golem attempted to enter the Wishing Grounds, but found itself repelled by a green barrier.

A small, glowing green sphere around the size of a baseball appeared before my eyes.

"Lord Touya!"

"Forest spirit? That you?"

"It is. I've currently focused most of my power on erecting a barrier, so please forgive my appearance. Could you use your power to evacuate the local tribes from the area? Their target is me, so please get the innocent bystanders out of here! They want to absorb the Wishing Tree, to infuse a Wood Golem with my spiritual power!" If a Wood Golem consumed the Wishing Tree it would probably be able to control the power of a forest spirit. It was likely that they'd made preparations for this to happen for a while.

The people behind this were obviously the Rivet tribe. If they'd won the Pruning, they were going to poison the Wishing Tree and then assimilate it into one of their Golems after it was weakened... Or perhaps they planned to turn the Wishing Tree itself into a Golem. There was no point in pondering, either way.

But then, the Rauli tribe snatched away their victory, so they had to resort to another plan. And that was what resulted in the current situation... They didn't know when to give up. Or rather, they were too stupid to know.

...Moroha suddenly decided to dump all that information on me. I couldn't believe it. I'd seen the Rivet tribe the night before, so they must have been making preparations for this. I should've just defeated them all there and then.

I used [Fly] to swoop down and paralyze two members of the Rivet tribe. The spirit's power was focused on maintaining the barrier, so my magic worked just fine.

"Tell me now, what are they?"

"W-Wood Golems. Our tribe raised them from saplings... We had them feed on the life of nearby trees so they would become behemoths, thanks to the adjustments we made to them..."

"Adjustments?"

"We mixed various poisons and remedies together, soaked them into their bark... It was a long process to transform them. They should be able to drain the Wishing Tree, as well... Use the spirit's power, and with that power, the Rivet tribe will reign supreme over the Sea of Trees... Kuhuhu..." Well, it was exactly as Moroha had said.

Don't think you've won yet, asshole! It's time for us to put the hurt on you!

"[Gate]." I opened a portal in the sky, allowing a Frame Gear to fall out.

The Knight Baron fell from about one meter up in the air, but still managed to make a heavy crash as it landed in the Wishing Grounds. It held a sword in one hand, and the Fragarach equipment was fitted to it as well.

"Wh-What is that?!"

"Shut up. It's time to test out the new weapon. I'll shatter your stupid Golems, and your tribe's pride along with it!" The Rivet tribesman looked absolutely stupefied as I walked over to my Frame Gear. But suddenly, Yumina and Linze yelled out to me.

"Touya, let one of us do it."

"Huh? You wanna ride the Knight Baron?"

"Yes… Neither of us were able to do a thing. Not during the Yulong incident, or during the Pruning…"

Oh, that is true, isn't it…? We didn't need magic during the Yulong incident, and it was banned for the Pruning rounds…

Well, we will need to fight against the Phrase again at some point, and the Fragarach will allow people like Yumina and Linze to channel their magical power into a physical piece of weaponry… I wonder if they're prepared for it, though.

"Well, alright then. Please be careful, though! You can rely on me for support." I opened up another [Gate] and brought forth another Frame Gear. Though, this one was painted blue… It was equipped with a mace. It was actually Vice-Commander Norn's specialized Frame Gear, but having Linze or Yumina ride it wouldn't be a big deal.

Yumina climbed into the black one, while Linze took the blue. They started them up and synchronized their magical patterns with the equipment.

"…Start the magic tuning. Activate the primary slot."

"Got it! Primary slot engaged! Charging the Fragarach! Tuning's complete. No complications."

"…Nothing wrong here, either." I took a radio out of [**Storage**] and communicated with them both. Everything seemed fine for the time being.

"Yumina, you take the enemies on the right. Linze, you can handle the left. If you feel your magic weakening, remember that your engagement rings have surplus magical power stored in them."

"Got it."

"R-Roger!" The Black Knight and Blue Knight made a running start, turning toward their respective Golems with weapons in hand.

"**Strike true, Lightning! Hundredspear Thunderclap: [Lightning Javelin]!**"

"**Pierce, o Ice! Frozen Point: [Ice Needle]!**" The Black Knight fired lightning from its sword, and the Blue Knight's mace became imbued with spines of ice. Then, they unleashed attacks upon the Golems.

Yumina was using a wind spell, which made sense, but Linze was clearly being mindful. Her best element was fire, but she probably didn't want the trees to ignite. Lightning was dangerous and could cause fires ordinarily, but magically created lightning didn't have any such side effects.

Two Golems fell beneath their assault, and the two rushed out from the Wishing Grounds.

"Don't overdo it, but I'd like you two to test out the Fragarach's capabilities. Just be wary." The two of them fanned out to meet more of the oncoming Wood Golems, but Yumina made her move first.

"Fragarach, activate!"

Four crystal blades began floating around the back of the Black Knight. Then, they moved forward, deploying out and orbiting the Frame Gear.

"Go!" As if responding to Yumina's cry, the crystal blades smashed into a Wood Golem at supersonic speed. It was splintered apart in seconds. The Fragarach was designed to be tough enough to smash the Phrase, so wood was nothing.

The blades shredded the Wood Golem's core and returned to orbit the Black Knight, floating freely in a circular pattern. They worked as a defensive system too, since they were based on the Satellite Orbs of Babylon.

"Hm... Is it difficult to target more than one enemy at the same time?"

"It is! I don't think it's impossible, but it's hard to focus quickly enough. I think with experience it'll become easier to handle." That made sense. Rosetta had spoken to me about rhythm and tempo, and how important it was to get accustomed to the beat of battle. It could definitely be compared to learning how to play an instrument. It was similar in effect, too. Like when you played the piano and made your left and right hands do different things.

I could actually manipulate all four Fragarach swords with ease, but I probably had my parents to thank for that. They made me play piano as a child. I never thought it would make me a more efficient combatant.

That reminded me that I hadn't seen a single piano in this world. I made a mental note to make one later, as it could help with learning how to control weapon systems like this. Also, I wanted to play the piano, since it had been too long.

"Fragarach, launch…"

Linze's Fragarach fired up and began tearing up her opposition. Unlike Yumina, however, two of her blades were moving at once.

Linze was able to attack two targets at the same time. Still, her movements were far less precise than they would have been if she just attacked with all four at once on the same target. It would surely improve with practice.

"Th-This is impossible… How…?!" A member of the Rivet tribe stared on in horror as his beautiful Golems were turned into hunks of bark.

I actually totally forgot about those guys. I targeted every member of the Rivet tribe on my map app, and hit the good old fashioned [**Paralyze**] switch. It was pretty easy to locate them, since they looked so distinct and all.

Most of the Golems were dead at this point. If they were made from mithril or orichalcum, we would've made serious money today. Regardless of whether or not they were selectively refined, wood was just wood at the end of the day. There wasn't any value to them in terms of raw material. Well, maybe they were good for fire kindling or something.

"There, all done." Linze took out the last remaining one. Every Golem had fallen. All the tribes in the Wishing Grounds cheered and celebrated upon seeing that victory had come. Well, all the tribes except the Rivet tribe, anyway.

But the trees in the vicinity had taken considerable damage. They were all extremely ancient trees too, judging from the sizes.

The spherical spirit came close to me once more. She had probably used up a lot of her energy on the barrier, so it'd be a bit before she could take human form again.

"Thank you, Lord Touya... How can I ever repay you?"

"No need... Actually, I should say sorry for trashing the trees around here. I could've done better."

"Not at all... I will focus my energy later on and restore them to how they were."

Oh? You can do that? Well, I guess you are a forest spirit after all...

The spirit suddenly whooshed over to the Judgment Tribe's spokesman, and looked to be communicating with him.

After a while, the man raised his voice.

"These malignant men schemed to make the Wishing Tree their own, but their ambitions have since been trampled! Envoys of Brunhild, a far-off nation, have protected us and our dear home! We, the tribes of the Sea of Trees, now offer unto them our deepest gratitude! May the spirit's blessing be with them, always!"

"May the spirit's blessing be with them, always!" As everyone clapped and cheered, I sent the two Frame Gears back home. Yumina and Linze were formally recognized as the saviors from Brunhild, and thus acted as our representatives to the Sea of Trees. That was fine by me, though. They were the ones that killed the Wood Golems anyway.

The members of the Jaja tribe rounded up all of the Rivet tribesmen, then took them away somewhere. I also asked them to round up the other Rivet tribesmen all over the Sea of Trees, since my mass paralysis should've affected everyone in the forest related to them.

Thus, the Rauli tribe was formally declared the Tribe of the Treelord, and their new law of separating the Pruning by gender was accepted.

The rule caused some confusion and chatter amongst most of the other tribes, but it was accepted by the forest spirit and put into effect.

The rule wasn't all that bad once I really thought about it, and the other tribes seemed to feel the same as well. It benefited everyone, as it was just another opportunity for victory. Though nothing would change for the Balm tribe. They didn't have women.

Still, they seemed to accept the ruling, saying that they were happy they'd never have to face off against the irritating Rauli tribe ever again.

Thus ended our foray into the Sea of Trees, and our very turbulent Pruning experience.

"Guh… It's cold! When did it get so cold?!" We were away for only three days, but Brunhild was colder than ever. It was hard to even get up in the morning.

The Sea of Trees was directly to our south, but it wasn't cold there in the winter. I couldn't tell if I was cold because I was used to the climate there, or if it had just actually gotten colder.

The climate of this world didn't operate on conventional logic. Seasons didn't exist everywhere, and where they did exist, they were often extreme. What seasons happened in which places also had nothing to do with geographical placement. There were small differences between east and west climates, however. That reminded me that I had no idea if the world was even spherical... It could've been flat. Hell, there might've even been a giant elephant or snake holding this world up.

Apparently spirits controlled the climate, but I didn't really know the details. I had no idea if it was related to magic, where magic even came from, or what. A country with four functional yearly seasons could be right next to a country where winter never ended. There was no rhyme or reason to it at all.

I didn't know if it was due to luck or what, but Brunhild had four distinct seasons. The environment was generally pretty similar to how it was where I grew up.

"I could really use a heater right about now..." It wouldn't even be that hard to make one using [**Program**], but it wasn't like the cold was unbearable or anything. Plus, we had a fireplace. My grandad used to say that "inconvenience itself is a form of energy," but I was digressing a bit. A hot water bottle would be fine. The Pruning was officially over, and Pam had given up on making a baby with me. She looked a bit sad, though.

I wanted her to prove herself as a member of the Rauli tribe, or rather, a member of the Tribe of the Treelord.

Brunhild had been formally recognized as a savior of the Sea of Trees, and they pledged to support us if anything ever happened. All the tribes agreed to lend their strength to me, should I ever need it.

I didn't get the full story about what happened to the Rivet tribe after that. Pam just told me that "the Sea of Trees passed judgment on them" and left it at that. I decided I probably didn't want to ask anything else about it.

I went out to the cold air of the balcony, only to see someone practicing in the training grounds. I couldn't see them too well though, since the air was heavy in the morning.

I used [**Long Sense**] to peek on them, and I saw Moroha sparring with someone. It was Lu.

"Man, so early, too…" It was probably because of her loss. Lu was angry that she was defeated by Rengetsu. She put on a brave face, but I knew better. My fiancees hated to lose.

Everyone in the castle was pretty surprised when I came home with Moroha. But that was only natural, since I'd never mentioned having another sister before.

Kousaka asked me how many siblings I had, and I gave him an ambiguous kind of answer… But I think he misunderstood me, because he gave me this kind of knowing nod as if to say "That many, huh…?" Thus, the idea that the Mochizuki lineage was a bloodline of womanizers became accepted.

That's not it, damn it! We aren't a bunch of siblings from different mothers! They aren't even my siblings!

What surprised them even more was Moroha's martial prowess. We showcased her skills by letting her duke it out with the knight order. It was a battle of her versus eighty. She won easily. Didn't get a scratch on her.

She also pointed out every soldier's individual weaknesses and gave them pointers to focus on. She was nothing if not meticulous.

"…Yep, you're the grand duke's sister alright." I asked Moroha to spar with the knight order whenever she had the free time. If they trained with her, then they'd likely become stronger over time. That was certainly a benefit, overall.

"Morning!"

"Good morning, Touya." I got changed and headed into the dining room. Yumina, Linze, Elze, Yae, Hilde, and Karen were sitting and waiting for me. I was feeling a bit drowsy, so Renne brought me a cup of herbal tea.

I said thanks to Renne and gave her a little pat on the head, when suddenly the door opened. It was Moroha and Lu, returning from their training.

We ate breakfast at seven in the morning, every morning. Though we didn't all have to be present to start eating. Still, if it was possible, we did enjoy eating together. Due to that, we usually ended up not actually starting to eat until after seven. Everyone was here today, even Karen, who usually liked to sleep in late.

Sue came to join us for breakfast now and then, but it seemed she was busy today.

Her room in the Ortlinde household was connected to my gateway room, so she could come and go as she pleased. Naturally only Sue was capable of accessing that particular portal, and it was set to record whenever she passed on through.

I was engaged to her, so she was allowed to come to Brunhild castle at her own discretion. Though, I did tell her to try and eat with her parents at home as much as she could.

It was better for parents to eat meals with their children. I didn't want Duke Ortlinde to feel lonely or sad.

After breakfast, we all set about our various businesses. Yae, Hilde, and Moroha all joined the knights to train. Yumina and Lu went to speak with old man Naito about the urban planning. Elze went to train, and Linze went to investigate the selectively bred crops. Karen, on the other hand, stayed in her room and did weird love god stuff. Basically, we did what we wanted or needed to do.

I didn't ever force my fiancees to do anything official, but it seemed that they liked helping with my affairs.

My plan for the day involved meeting with anyone that requested an audience. If nobody did, then I'd have some free time. I listened to Kousaka prattle on about domestic issues here and there, dividing them between urgent, non-urgent, and unimportant matters.

Kousaka constantly tried to solve issues using the citizens, even though I could solve those issues in seconds flat, but he was right to do so. If I handled everything, the country would just rely on me forever. If the country couldn't stand on its own, then it couldn't really be called a country. I wasn't going to be around forever.

So whenever I offered to help out, Kousaka saw me as more of a hindrance than a help. Still, it was comfy not having any responsibilities.

"How much colder will it get, I wonder…"

"Hm… I don't believe we'll get any colder this year, sir. Even if it does, the Hot Carpet you created is a mighty boon to us all in the cold season." Laim, my butler, spoke up as he brought me my black tea. There were a lot of big rooms in the castle, so keeping the whole place warm was a pain. That was why I enchanted various carpets with the fire spell [**Warming**] and placed them all over the castle.

I also gave Laim a specially tailored suit enchanted with the spell. It was a great suit because it regulated its own temperature. Laim was very stiff, so I didn't think he'd take the gift if I just offered him it. That was why I used his upcoming birthday as a convenient excuse to force it upon him.

I didn't want our butler to get sick, after all.

I had plenty of free time, since nobody wanted to see me. Well, I wasn't completely free. I had decided to spend my time finishing off the piano I'd started to make after coming back from the Sea of Trees.

Building the piano wasn't too hard. It was basically just a huge outward fake thing. I'd gone and used [**Program**] to jury rig the aspects I didn't quite understand. The only issue was tuning it. I had to manually determine the tone using a piano app on my smartphone.

Even so, I got pretty excited and wound up making an eighty-eight key grand piano. It might have been better if I'd made a sixty-five key studio upright piano, but it was too late.

I wasn't one hundred percent sure, but I'd finished tuning it for the time being. I sat down on the chair and ran my finger along the keys. *Do, re, mi, fa, sol, la, ti, do.* I played them in order, and then backward. *Do, ti, la, sol, fa, mi, re, do.*

How long has it been since I last played… When I was a little kid, I couldn't get to fa using my thumb. I don't remember how I practiced… but I remember struggling to hit mi with my middle finger… My fingers were pretty short back then, huh.

I began to play the nostalgic tune of do, re, mi, fa, sol, la, ti, do, followed by do, ti, la, sol, fa, mi, re, do. I repeated it a few times for good measure.

After getting into the flow, I began to play Der Flohwalzer. I got a little excited about it and ended up doing a few different arrangements. I ended up playing a jazzier version, too.

After I was finished playing, I heard someone clapping. I turned around to see Sakura. She was standing alongside Kougyoku.

"Is that… an instrument?"

"Yeah, it is. It's called a piano. It's a keyboard instrument… but it could be classed as a percussion or string instrument too."

"I'd like to hear more. Another tune…"

Hm... Let's see. I'll go with another easy one. It's been a while since I've played this one, but here goes nothing... I can't think of a better song for this season.

I began to play, a slow tempo guiding me. It was a traditional Christmas tune. Still, I didn't know if the month of December existed in this world.

The song was Jingle Bells.

Something told me that the American man who came up with this song over a hundred and fifty years ago would never have dreamed it'd be played in another world.

Sakura bobbed her head gently from left to right. She seemed to enjoy it. Kougyoku closed her eyes too, as if appreciating the melody. They both started humming along to the tune of the song.

When I was finished, she clapped softly again. I felt a little bashful.

"The song... Teach me. I'd like to sing it." Sakura asked me, glimmering puppy dog eyes trained on my face. It was pretty unusual of her to be acting like this. She was normally so emotionally withdrawn.

Still, I answered her request and played the song once more, this time singing the lyrics along with the melody. Sakura hummed along as I sang. Once I was finished, I told her I'd do it again, but she told me that she'd already memorized all the lyrics. That was weird.

I started to play the tune again, and this time Sakura was the one singing. *W-Whoa... What the heck?!* She was... amazing. Her voice was clear, unwavering, and beautiful. I had no idea she had this kind of talent in her. When she finished, she smiled broadly and seemed very happy.

"Incredible... Do you think you might've been a singer?"

"I'm not sure about that, but I may have liked to sing. Could you show me more?" I wondered if it might help her memories return, so I started lining up all the songs I could think of. Pop, rock, folk, nursery rhymes. Western or Japanese, that didn't matter too much.

Incredibly, she memorized song lyrics despite only hearing them once. Her memory was astounding. Ironic, given the fact that she had amnesia.

Still, that voice of hers could be a formidable weapon through which to make a living. I could probably become an idol producer for her or something... Or at least, if she wasn't such a naturally withdrawn person.

The piano I had right now wasn't built for accompanying singers, so I figured I should make a better one. To be honest, I was a little concerned about teaching Yumina and the others how to play, since I wasn't even sure if this would help them manipulate the Fragarach.

It didn't take long for others to hear Sakura's incredible notes echoing throughout the castle. Before I knew it, we'd gathered quite an audience.

A torrent of applause came down upon us once she was finished. Sakura looked at the ground out of embarrassment, but she smiled gently when Linze gave her a few words of encouragement.

After that, we continued on with the mini-concert. She was a shy and reserved girl in many ways, but singing brought out another side of her that I hadn't seen before.

I continued to play for her, while making a mental note to download some songs to my smartphone for her to listen to.

"...ilde?"

"Hilde? Hilde!"

"Wha—?!" Hildegard, First Princess of the Knight Kingdom of Lestia, yelled out in response to her brother's voice suddenly permeating her consciousness.

"B-B-B-Brother dearest, why must you scream out of nowhere?"

"It wasn't out of nowhere!"

"You know how many times I called you? It's like your mind is somewhere else and you just can't concentrate, right?"

"Are you dissatisfied that I took the throne?"

"Preposterous! I was just thinking about something." While Hilde grew flustered at her brother Reinhard's remarks, the council room was enveloped in snickering.

They were in the council room for the knight order, the symbol of Lestia.

Currently, the knight order was separated into twelve squadrons with Hilde serving as squad leader for the third. Incidentally, Hilde's brother was serving as the squad leader of the first squadron.

In the land of Lestia, the king serves as the head of the knight order. This tradition came from the first king who proclaimed, "They who are worthy of being known as king must stand on the vanguard, protect their subjects, and lead them to glory."

The man who stood as the head of the knight order was the father of both Hilde and her brother, the king, Reid Yunas Lestia, though he would be resigning soon.

And the current prince would inherit his throne.

In other words, the new head of the knight order would be Reinhard.

The purpose of today's council was to determine who would fill the gap left by him as the new leader of the first squadron.

"Engrossing yourself such that you lose sight of your surroundings is both one of your strong points and flaws. Though, it was inappropriate to bring up such a topic in this setting. Please change topics."

"Sheesh… No need to tell me."

"Well, I won't go as far as to inquire into what you were thinking." Reinhard, nonchalantly as if nothing happened, shifted his gaze to the list of new candidates to be the head of the knight order.

Hilde sensed that Reinhard knew what she was truly feeling and became a bit embarrassed.

She cleared her throat, and with new found guise of composure, followed her brother's example and turned her gaze to the list of candidates.

For a short while she listened intently to the squadron heads' recommendations, but her eyes wandered to the sword at her hip.

There were only three crystal swords in this land. Her father had another and her grandfather the last. Its ability to cut struck fear into people's hearts. It was seen as either a blade of the gods, or a sword from the pits of hell. Even Holy Sword Lestia, the sword which had been passed down from generation to generation through the royal family, paled in comparison.

The event from that time popped into her mind from the depths of her memories. The memory of the boy that valiantly appeared when she was attacked by the monsters that were immune to both sword and magic. The boy that saved her from the brink of despair.

As she recalled the event, her chest began to warm.

First came the feeling of relief from being saved. After he went off on his merry way, she gained the desire to grow stronger in order to wipe away the feeling of incompetence that developed due to her weakness. At the same time, she developed an interest in the kind of man the boy was.

She found it very fortuitous that she was able to listen to the story of the grand duke of Brunhild from a merchant that she'd encountered on the way back to the castle.

Hilde didn't just hear of his strength, but also his disposition. And so, her interest increased.

Slaying Dragons, exterminating Golems, and ending a coup, indeed his force was one to be reckoned with, but there was more. His philanthropic activity ranged widely: he offered rare materials to aid in the reconstruction of the Mismede town that had been ravaged by a Dragon, and created institutions so that the common man could learn to read.

Hilde began feeling a sense of aspiring to be like that boy blossom inside her.

"…ilde. Hilde? Hilde!"

"Wha—?!" Yet again her brother's voice yanked her out of the sea of contemplation. Reinhard's expression formed into one of frustration, which was to be expected since this same sequence had played out twice already.

"I apologize." Hilde shrank and spent the rest of the council meeting in a state of discomfort.

"Ah… I sure messed up." Hilde sighed. This had been happening nonstop recently. She couldn't cheer up at all.

Though Hilde knew why it was happening, she had no idea what to do about it.

"Ah?!" Hilde heard a scream nearby.

"Ohohohoho…" A hearty laugh echoed from the same direction as the scream.

"Oh, Grandfather." If you heard a woman's scream in this castle, there was an eighty percent chance that it was the work of the former king. Hilde figured that the scream most likely came from a new maid that started just the other day.

And just as she expected, the previous king, her grandfather, approached Hilde from across the hallway with cane in hand. He was in such great condition that he didn't even need a cane, but he insisted on maintaining his image.

"Hello, Hilde. You look a tad down in the dumps."

"Please leave me be…" The girl wanted to yell at her grandfather, express her suffering. Express that, unlike him, she had real fears to contend with, but she also didn't want to lash out.

With no energy to hang around her unreasonably cheery grandfather, Hilde trudged past him.

"Hey now, hold your horses. A letter just came from the guild."

"From the guild…?" Her grandfather was one of the only two in the world: a former adventurer of the highest rank, Gold. He had deep ties with the guild, and was able to acquire information here and there.

"Don't be startled. Yulong has fallen."

"What?! Yulong did?!" Hilde raised her voice. He told her not to be startled, but how couldn't she be?

Yulong, Empire of Heaven. The only nation in all of the east that could rival Lestia.

Hilde wasn't too fond of the land of Yulong.

Predicated on the reason that Yulongese merchants tried to deceive people. Many of them seemed to believe that the fooled were at fault and idiotic.

And they had no concerns about telling such short-sighted lies. When a Yulongese person was caught committing crimes, they rarely admitted fault.

Say for instance you were to catch a thief. They would tell you that the shop they stole from was asking for it. They behaved as if those they harmed were the assailants and they themselves were the victims. Even then, they still got on their high horses, quibbled in the most obnoxious ways, and still had the audacity to say others were at fault. Hilde was upset by how self-centered they were as a people.

And their homeland knew of these deeds but wouldn't attempt to lay a finger on them. They simply pretended not to see. There were far too many government officials receiving bribes from the merchants, so they didn't think it was immoral.

Their logic was that everyone else did it as well, so what was wrong with doing it? Since others were getting away with it, they may as well do it themselves. They reasoned that they'd rather take advantage than be taken advantage of.

Thus, Lestia refused to engage in trade relations with the merchants or their government. No matter how sweet the deal may have seemed, they'd vowed to always decline their offer.

The Shady Land. That was the essence of Yulong.

That very Yulong had fallen. Yulong was in fact actually a military state. It relied on its overwhelming numbers to crush smaller neighboring countries.

They would do anything to achieve victory. Assassinate, betray, and ambush, all was fair to them in love and war. The people of Lestia held the concept of 'fair and square' in high esteem, which gave them another reason to not be able to accept the Yulongese.

"Who were they attacked by? No way, are you telling me it was Xenoahs?"

"No, that's incorrect. They were not taken down by another land. You should know as well. It was the Phrase."

"The Phrase!" Hilde would never forget those crystal creatures. The monsters that disgraced her for her lack of power.

"The news is that there was a swarm of thousands of them that attacked Yulong. Amongst their ranks was one that was about as big as a castle and the mysterious light it expelled from its mouth decimated the capital Shenghai."

"Unbelievable!"

"Indeed. Now I'm going to get to the main point. Someone exterminated the entire swarm that eliminated the city. The grand duke of Brunhild. It seems that he found a relic from an ancient civilization. It was some kind of army of giants that he activated and used to exterminate the swarm."

"Are you serious?!" Hilde raised her voice louder than that time just a little while ago. And that was because he had mentioned the man who'd been on her mind for the longest time. It was an unavoidable outcome.

Hilde heard everything from her grandfather from start to finish. The grand duke of Brunhild cooperated with other lands that he had amicable relations with and formed an alliance that led to the defeat of the invading Phrase.

In addition, he didn't expect any collateral from Yulong or steal any land.

Just as expected from His Highness the Duke. Hilde was really impressed at his incredible ability to shoulder a country at such a young age, but adults seemed to have dissenting opinions.

"Personally, I think it's frightening for a single man to have such power. If the duke is so inclined, he can wipe a country or two off of the face of the planet. Even our very own land of Lestia. Hilde... what did you think of the man in question when you met him?" The former king shifted his gaze over to Hilde. With a hint of hesitation in her voice, Hilde told him how she really felt from her heart.

"I felt that he was a polite man with an upstanding personality. He doesn't hesitate in lending out a helping hand to those in need... Rather, he does it as if it were the obvious thing to do. That is my opinion of him."

"I see..." She'd only met him once. The conversation they had only lasted a few minutes. How could she say she knew anything about him just from that? She realized that her speech was just her desire for how she wished he was.

"I have the faintest idea of what kind of relationship we should form with the Duke. Some say that the invasion of the Phrase was all orchestrated by him so he could clean it up himself. A one-man show. Others say that they saw him summon them."

"That's ridiculous! That's obviously a lie! You know that's the kind of tactic Yulong always uses!"

"Indeed. I also suspected the same thing. They'd use this as an opportunity to appeal to the world of them being victims of the Duchy and demand reparations and his giant warriors. That land is the same as ever, blackmailing and extorting." The former king whispered as he stroked his white beard. Lestia had met a similar fate in the past. The Yulongese claimed that five hundred years ago, Holy Sword Lestia was stolen from them. Though it went without question that Lestia paid them no heed, such rumors were frustrating for various reasons.

"Whatever the case may be, we must decide on a course of action. And so… I shall be making my way to Brunhild and meeting with the duke himself to determine what his true intentions are."

"Whaaaaaat?!" Hilde gasped as her eyes shot wide open. The reason for her surprise was, of course, not the fact that the former king of Lestia, her grandfather, was going to head toward Brunhild, but the childish, egotistical thought that it wasn't fair that she was getting left out.

"I'm going too."

"Huh? Well, that's…"

"I'm going to go too! I'm going to go speak with father about this!" Hilde ran to her father, the king, without listening to her grandfather's response.

"…So, you're saying that you accompanied the preceding king against his will, you did? Is that summation apt?"

"Well uh… Yes… Something like that, I guess." Hilde forced a smile in response to Yae as she drank her tea.

A tea party was hosted at the castle terrace to deepen their friendship with Hilde, who was the most recently engaged girl.

Of course, the attendees other than Hilde were Yumina, Elze, Linze, Yae, Sue, and Lu. Their fiance Touya was absent.

Gatherings with only these ladies happened rather frequently. While they served to deepen bonds, they also discussed how the other fiancees were doing, as well as exchanged perspectives on Touya.

"Touya gets strangely aggressive when I leave him alone." Such was Yumina's position.

"Speaking of which, is it okay for you to be here? Didn't you say you had an official position in the knight order?"

"Yes, though there's no need for concern. I made my replacement the candidate who got rejected when brother dearest's replacement was being chosen." Hilde responded to Elze's question with a smile. She was no longer a knight of Lestia, since she decided she'd serve Brunhild… Or rather, she'd chosen to be Touya's personal knight.

"Alright. Hilde can reside here. Though, I would really wish to reside here too…" Sue spoke with a pout as she petted Kohaku, who was sitting on her lap. Yumina chimed in, addressing her cousin.

"Sue. My uncle would be quite upset if you left home. Stay home a while longer, alright? You can come here whenever you wish, okay?"

"That is true… but I always end up thinking of Touya when I'm over there. I'm somewhat worried, but I think it's fine since Yumina is here. Touya's kind of a dunce." Though they thought that sentiment was quite harsh, everyone except for Hilde nodded deeply in agreement.

Nobody had the slightest clue what he'd get into if they took their eyes off him for a second. He'd become acquaintances with some strange fellows, get himself involved in something totally absurd, or build something incomprehensible.

Even though his antics didn't result in a large quantity of victims arising, Hilde could feel her heart getting weaker and weaker each time he startled her.

"When was it again? When he made that weird box that washed clothes?"

"Oh… the washing machine? It just crumpled up all the clothes." Elze and Linze spoke of a strange contraption Touya had built. According to him, he miscalculated the amount of wind magic that would produce the optimal rotational strength. Using too much wind magic to generate the magical blade was the big mistake.

"Recently he made this weird hair blowing contraption that he calls the dryer. It was definitely a blunder, though…"

"It blew fire like a Dragon in a rage would, it did." Yae let out a sigh at Lu's impression. If Touya were there, he'd likely make the excuse that it was difficult to balance wind and fire magic.

"How does someone get that kind of idea?"

"Well, we are talking about Touya after all." While Elze wasn't too happy about Yumina's response to her, she more of less agreed with the sentiment.

Everyone other than Hilde probably shared the same opinion.

"Sorry to interrupt, but as the newest member I would feel most obliged if you would listen to my question."

"That's fine. What is it?" Elze reached for a potato chip as she replied to Hilde, whose demeanor could be best described as stiff. This meeting also functioned as Hilde's welcome party. Everyone intended to answer all questions that they could.

"How would you fine ladies describe Touya's parents? Since I became his fiancee, I think it may be suitable to introduce myself…"

"Ah, about that."

"The truth is, we've never actually met them ourselves."

"Really? D-Did his parents happen to pass away…?"

"I don't believe that's the case… but I'm not too certain since Touya doesn't seem like he wishes to speak of his family matters." It was obvious from Linze's facial expression that she was troubled. She felt a bit left out from the fact that she didn't even know his family's structure despite being engaged to him.

Even if she tried to get information out of him, she was met with a troubled face, and he evaded the topic. Linze and the others understood that rather than not wanting to say something about it, there was some hesitation that kept him from talking about it.

Upon hearing this, Hilde suddenly came to a realization. Since he had such overwhelming power, it wouldn't be strange for him to be estranged from his family. Great power could bring about great misfortune.

"He doesn't have the best relationship with…"

"Wrong answer! It's not that his family hates him. The situation's just a wee bit complicated. Explaining what's going on to you all would just be kind of hard is all. Just wait for him to be ready to talk about it." All members present, including the tiger, were startled to the point of basically jumping out of their seats at the sudden voice.

"D-D-D-Dear sister Karen?!" Touya's sister, Mochizuki Karen, found an open seat next to Lu, reached out for the potato chips, and began stuffing her face.

"When did you get here…?" Hilde wasn't able to hide her surprise at the fact that Karen went completely unnoticed. She was sitting back and relaxing as if she'd been sitting there the whole time, but rest assured, that seat was empty until just a second ago.

Hilde thought that she may have used transportation magic. It wouldn't have been odd for her to have similar abilities to her brother.

While Hilde had such ideas race through her mind, Karen sent a grin her way.

"There's no reason to rush, you know. He should tell you about it before long if you take the time to get to know him slowly."

"I see…"

"Well, you want to know everything about the person you love! I'm well aware of a damsel stricken with L-O-V-E. And that's where I step in! I'll give my cute widdle sisters the hot scoop, y'know?!'"

Everyone in the room's ear started violently twitching in response to Karen's words. Well, Kohaku's didn't.

Linze gulped as she sat straight across from Karen and opened her mouth.

"Wh-What kind of information?"

"Hehehe. I'll be an open book about the boy's first love during early childhood! How about that?!"

"F-First love?! Touya's?!" Yumina approached Karen, clearly going into a frenzy. It was safe to say that he had never said one word about that topic. Well, it would definitely have been off-putting hearing him boast about his first love to his fiancee.

There was no blood relation between Touya and Karen. Obviously, she didn't live with him during their early childhood, nor should she have any knowledge of his memories when it came to that. But in the end, Karen *was* the goddess of love.

There was nothing love-related beyond Karen's scope. She knew everything about Touya's life, at least the romantic aspects. She knew of the different types of girls he'd been into all the way to the first porno magazine he bought.

Karen looked around to each person there with a mischievous grin on her face.

"Wanna hear about it?"

"Absolutely!" They all nodded enthusiastically. That made the heavenly beast on Sue's lap, who was infinitely loyal to its master, begin to panic. After all, Touya's privacy was in grave danger.

Kohaku was aware of its ignorance regarding human sensibilities, but the tiger knew full well that it had to inform him of this.

It tried contacting him via telepathy, but alas, it didn't work. Baffled by this, Kohaku looked up and saw Karen give it a wink.

Though unaware of how she was doing it, the white tiger became absolutely certain that Karen was the one preventing it from contacting its master.

"Master, please forgive my powerlessness." Kohaku closed its eyes, completely dejected.

"Ah...choo!"

"Are you ill, Your Majesty?" Rubbing my nose, I told him that I was fine. It probably wasn't a cold or anything, but I had a strange chill go down my spine.

This has happened before, hasn't it? Well, whatever.

We'd opened up a part of the forest to build a large obstacle course.

It was both a place for children to play and a training ground for the knights to practice.

It was split into three courses: beginner, intermediate, and advanced. In other words, "for children, for adults, and for knights."

You'd have to go through the course by entering through my right and leaving through the left. The three courses were all semicircles built around a single point. The one inside was the one for children, the middle one was for adults, and the outer one for knights.

The one for children was a simple obstacle course with stone skipping, rope-climbing, log-crossing, etc. Basically, it was a place where they could train while having fun.

The adult obstacle course was harder, with rock climbing, spinning log-bridges, ropes you had to swing through like Tarzan, and so on.

As for the knight obstacle course...

"Uahhhhhh!"

"And that's the second time Logan has failed." Hearing the huge splash as something fell in the pond, Lain wrote a cross on the paper she had in her hands.

We were now testing the completed course. Well, it was done primarily by the knights who had confidence in their physical abilities.

"Shame. He got pretty far."

"Honestly, that would happen to anyone who had water poured on them while hanging to a wall."

"I was actually thinking of using oil at first."

"That's just evil," she mumbled under her breath.

Is it really? I think it's pretty normal to use oil, especially on the last stones in stone skipping or steep wall-climbing.

I'd made lots of varied obstacles. There were even some gravity zones, where the gravity was several times greater than normal.

Indeed, I had the knights try and make it through monkey bars in areas imbued with **[Gravity]**. However, the spell was so strong that not many of them made it through. *Hmm... This is training, so I don't know if I should weaken it. Yeah, I'll just keep it like this.*

"Gwaaah!"

And there goes another knight. He climbed out of the pond and mumbled something as he went back to the starting point.

"I get it now! I'll make it through next time…!"

"Just gotta put my mind to it!"

"Let's gooo!" It was nice to see them all fired up about it. Not like it would be enough for them to make it through, though.

"There's rolling stones, springing bridges, swinging guillotines… Are you sure this is safe?"

"I did design it so no one would end up hurt. The stones are light enough to not crush any bones, while the guillotines don't cut at all. They're just there to keep the people on their toes." I could see why Lain was worried, but unlike the children's course, this one wasn't a game. They were training here, and they had to be serious about it. A little bit of tenseness couldn't hurt.

"Uhyeeeaaaghhh!" With great momentum, a knight just dropped off the steep slope. He moved his arms as if swimming through the air, but that wasn't enough to land him on the safe zone, and he ended up in the pond below.

"He didn't have enough momentum. Well, that always happens when you're scared of the speed."

"…Is this course even possible?"

"Well, I cleared it."

"You shouldn't be used as the standard, Your Majesty." Lain breathed a long sigh.

Eeeh…? The knights continued trying to clear the course until it was nearly evening, when Nikola reached the end, all tattered and torn.

See? It's possible.

When he went down from the goal, the knights all ran up to him and raised him up high, cheering loudly.

"He did it! He actually did it!"

"We've won!"

"We've cleared the demon's course!"

"Hail the vice captain!"

Hey, who are you calling a demon? That's rude.

In all honestly, I was a bit vexed that someone was able to clear it. I decided that I might have to enhance it later down the line.

Though, I guess I should keep it like this until everyone's able to do it.

With the training done, I returned back to the castle, where the girls all came out to greet me, but...

"W-Welcome back, Touya-kun!"

"'Touya-kun'?" Yumina, who always called me just "Touya," was now speaking to me with a familiar honorific.

"W-Welcome back home, Touya-kun."

"Well done on the t-training, Touya-kun."

"Lu? Linze?" Those two were also acting strange.

Hell, they *looked* strange, too. Though a bit different in design, they were all wearing school uniforms... The sailor type. And it suited them all pretty well, too.

"Hey, Yae! Y-You go first!"

"Please wait! I-I am not accustomed to looking like this, I am not! The skirt is too short!"

"I-I'm not used to wearing skirts, either, so...!" Elze, Yae, and Hilde were all fighting over something behind the pillar.

What are you all doing?

They all seemed to have caught some sailor uniform infection. Was there some sort of boom I missed?

"Oh! Touya, you're back! Do you like how we look?"

"You too, Sue? What's going on here?" She was also wearing a sailor uniform. And for some reason, she had some machine gun-like toy.

It was cute, but in her case, it felt like she was made to wear it, and it almost seemed like some sort of cosplay. The others were the appropriate age, so the uniforms seemed very fitting.

"You like this clothing, don't you? We look just like your first love, Shoko!"

"...UH?" My mind went blank.

Excuse me? Shoko, as in, *that* Shoko? There was only one person she could be referring to, and that would be the older girl that lived next to me when I was younger.

And did she say "first love"? How did she know that?!

"W-We can't become older than you, but we can look like her, at the very least…" Yumina said that with her face red to her ears.

Wait, wait, wait! That's why they're wearing those?! Well, it's true that Shoko went to a school that used sailor uniforms, but…!

"Alright, hold on…! Umm, wh-who told you about Shoko…?"

"Karen did."

"THAT GODDAMN IDIOT!"

The hell are you telling them?! Why'd you reveal my secret like that?! I've never told anyone!

"Wh-What else did she tell you…?"

"What else? Ehm…"

"Like the fact that you went to see her every single day."

"Or that you tried to get her attention with flowers you picked from the park."

"Or that you cried when you found out that she was moving."

"Oaaagh…" I fell down to my knees on the carpet-covered floor. *What kind of punishment is this?!* That had happened before I was even in elementary school! And such youthful indiscretions surely weren't that uncommon! Also, I'd heard that she got married by the time I was in middle school.

I wonder if she's happy. No, wait, that doesn't matter right now. What matters is the embarrassing reality that my first love was revealed. Damn, I want to crawl into a hole and die...

"Umm... does it look bad on us?"

"...No, not at all. You all look adorable." I threw a thumbs up toward Linze, making the worry in her face vanish.

They were probably made in Zanac's place, and it surprised me that they had so many versions. Summer clothes, winter clothes... and Yumina's pure white sailor uniform must've been pretty rare. *Were there some cosplay outfits among the normal uniforms? Did I really give them all that many designs...? Well, I wasn't really paying attention when I ran a search on my smartphone and used* [**Drawing**] *on whatever I got.*

Gh... I really do enjoy seeing them all in sailor uniforms, but that stupid sister of mine deserves some serious punishment.

"Touya? Why is my cake so small?!"

"Who knows? Maybe you've been a bad girl." Feigning ignorance, I continued eating my own shortcake. Unlike the others, Karen's shortcake was so small that there was a question as to if it could hold a strawberry.

Of course, I was the one who cut it. And obviously, my own portion was all the more bigger for it.

Feel the resentment of my damaged privacy.

As I calmly ate my cake, Karen directed her fork in my direction and moved it with the speed of a shooting star. It was aimed at the large strawberry on my plate.

"Like hell!" With a satisfying, metallic sound, I used my own fork to stop hers. Apparently, her rightfully-earned cake wasn't enough, so she took to taking more from the others.

"A little brother should be considerate of his elder sister, y'know?!"

"An elder sister shouldn't take things from her little brother!"

"Please calm down, you two." As we glared at each other, Yumina broke up the fight.

"We girls will share our cake with you, Karen, so come eat with us."

"That's Yumina for you!"

Damn it, she doesn't deserve that! She was a person who would keep doing stupid stuff until someone severely punished her. Well, a "god," rather than a "person," but still. I hoped she could at least act in a manner deserving of the title. Perhaps I had to tell on her to the World God.

Karen ate Yumina's cake with the most blissful expression imaginable.

"You're all such good girls. I think I should let you in on a little secret."

"A secret?"

"The first erotic book that Touya ever had was—"

"HOLD IT RIGHT THERE! THE HELL ARE YOU SAYING?! COULD YOU PLEASE STOP ALREADY?!" I went behind her and closed her mouth.

Goddamn, this is annoying! Gods are such a pain in the ass!

Following that exchange, I told her that if she kept leaking my private information, she wouldn't be getting any more sweets. She got teary-eyed and cried "Not the sweets!" so I figured I was safe in that regard.

Having such a childish god as a relative sure is annoying…

The Dragon Knight
《DRAGOON》

Developer: Regina Babylon   Chief Engineer: ???
Maintainer: ???   Affiliation: Ende
Compatible Pilots: Ende.

Height: 17.8m   Weight: 6.8t   Maximum Capacity: 1 Person
Armaments: Twin Crystal Blades

One of the Anti-Phrase Weapons, a Frame Gear. Built for speed, its armor is exceptionally lightweight,
resulting in mediocre defensive capabilities. It can lower its heels to move around on a set of wheels.
By shifting forms this way it can reach extreme speeds. Though difficult to handle, attacking in this Frame Gear
is optimally done through a "hit and run" tactic of moving in towards the enemy, slicing at them,
and then retreating at high speeds.

Well, here we are again. Volume seven of In Another World With My Smartphone.

This volume sure was action-packed, huh? This volume's longer than usual, so the afterword's smaller in turn. Thanks for understanding. Once again, Eiji Usatsuka... Thank you for your illustrations as usual. I look forward to seeing what you produce next. Thanks to you as well, Tomofumi Ogasawara, for the Frame Gear designs. You've been busy as ever.

K, the Hobby Japan Editorial Department, and everyone else involved in publishing the book, you have my appreciation.

Thanks again to everyone who supports my story on Shōsetsuka ni Narō.

Oh, that reminds me, I'm really excited because a manga version of this story will start publication in Comp Ace on November 26th, 2016! Thank you so much...

— Patora Fuyuhara

Patora Fuyuhara
illustration·Eiji Usatsuka

VOLUME 8
ON SALE
FEBRUARY 2020!

In Another World With My Smartphone

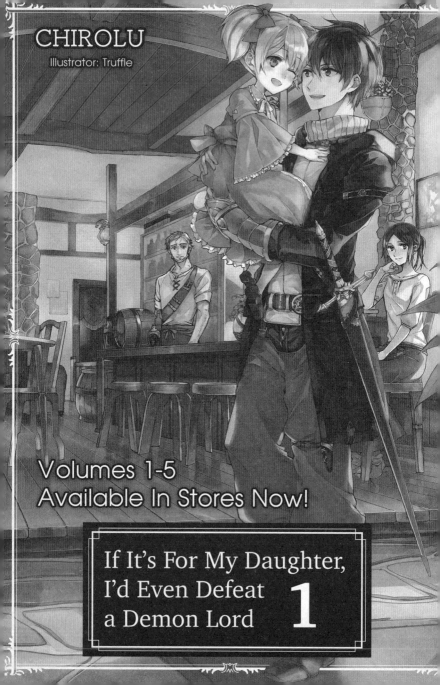

amei Hitsuji
stration=himesuz

The Magic in This Other
World is Too Far Behind!
Volumes 1-6 Available Now!

VOLUMES 1-6
ON SALE NOW!

How NOT to Summon a Demon Lord

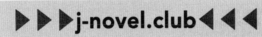

J-Novel Club Lineup

Ebook Releases Series List

Amagi Brilliant Park
An Archdemon's Dilemma: How to Love Your Elf Bride
Ao Oni
Arifureta Zero
Arifureta: From Commonplace to World's Strongest
Bluesteel Blasphemer
Brave Chronicle: The Ruinmaker
Clockwork Planet
Demon King Daimaou
Der Werwolf: The Annals of Veight
ECHO
From Truant to Anime Screenwriter: My Path to "Anohana" and "The Anthem of the Heart"
Gear Drive
Grimgar of Fantasy and Ash
How a Realist Hero Rebuilt the Kingdom
How NOT to Summon a Demon Lord
I Saved Too Many Girls and Caused the Apocalypse
If It's for My Daughter, I'd Even Defeat a Demon Lord
In Another World With My Smartphone
Infinite Dendrogram
Infinite Stratos
Invaders of the Rokujouma!?
JK Haru is a Sex Worker in Another World
Kokoro Connect
Last and First Idol
Lazy Dungeon Master
Me, a Genius? I Was Reborn into Another World and I Think They've Got the Wrong Idea!
Mixed Bathing in Another Dimension
My Big Sister Lives in a Fantasy World
My Little Sister Can Read Kanji
My Next Life as a Villainess: All Routes Lead to Doom!
Occultic;Nine
Outbreak Company
Paying to Win in a VRMMO
Seirei Gensouki: Spirit Chronicles
Sorcerous Stabber Orphen: The Wayward Journey
The Faraway Paladin
The Magic in this Other World is Too Far Behind!
The Master of Ragnarok & Blesser of Einherjar
The Unwanted Undead Adventurer
Walking My Second Path in Life
Yume Nikki: I Am Not in Your Dream